Dr. Lubin's guide helps women facin̲ ... ... you. She provides practical and "doa... talk, managing anxiety, and improvi... you through your diagnosis, treatment, and healing, but also teach you self-care lessons to improve your everyday life beyond breast cancer.

Salud Astrud
Six-Year Breast Cancer Survivor
President Board of Directors
Virginia Breast Cancer Foundation

Dr. Lubin has devoted her career and heart to helping women with breast cancer navigate their journey. Now she has poured her vast knowledge, experience, compassion, and love into this book so that any woman who has had breast cancer or faced another life-altering trauma—and those who love them—can benefit. Packed with affirming anecdotes, healing exercises, tips, and "ah-ha" moments, it will help you reflect on your own journey and find its meaning within your own life. Read this book—you'll feel Dr. Lubin is speaking directly to you!

René Bowditch and Mary Beth Gibson
Founders of Here for the Girls, Inc. (H4TG)
A non-profit supporting young women with breast cancer

Dr. Lubin continues to be a trailblazer in the fight for wellness beyond a breast cancer diagnosis. This is evident in her first book. This complete interactive workbook is a must-have as a survivor begins their journey toward wholeness. It challenges, encourages, and inspires. I assure you Dr. Lubin did not read your journal or listen in on your prayer. She studied the profound impact this diagnosis has on women and used her professionalism to create a survivors' bible. Wellness is multifaceted, and she understands that. If you desire to move beyond existing to thriving, this is the book for you.

Clayres Johnson BSN, RN, CBCN
Oncology Nurse Navigator
McLeskey Comprehensive Breast Center

What a godsend! Finally, somebody gets it! Dr. Lubin understands the pitfalls of a medical system whose emphasis on physical recovery can overlook the mental and spiritual costs of a very disempowering disease. This compassionate guide gives you straight solutions for regaining control over medical situations that can flood you with their complexity and uncertainty. With Dr. Lubin's effective tools, you can stop the overwhelm and restore hope. Let her show you how to make each phase of your challenge a chance to live your best life and find meaning in the process.

Lindsay C. Gibson, PsyD
Clinical psychologist and author of *Adult Children of Emotionally Immature Parents.*

... An authoritative guide to navigating your breast cancer journey. Dr. Lubin weaves forty years of practice together with science in an easy-to-understand conversation. With compassion and deep respect for privacy, she tells stories of women who have traveled this path and taught her many lessons. In this "interactive manual" she journeys with the patient, providing research-based information, tutorials, and step-by-step exercises in many areas of life including sexuality and spirituality. This book is every sojourner's guide to healing.

Stonsa Insinna, PhD
Clinical Psychologist and Registered Nurse

Medical professionals heal the physical side of breast cancer. So who helps heal the emotional side? Dr. Lubin brings her insight and understanding to the cancer experience and to topics that are often overlooked in the medical setting. This guide helps you recognize the emotional difficulties most cancer patients encounter and then equips you with tools to empower yourself to control what you can. She normalizes your concerns so that you feel less alone and better armed to take responsibility for your own wellbeing. This incredibly helpful book should be recommended to anyone going through a diagnosis of breast cancer.

Belinda Risher MS, RN, CBCN
Oncology Nurse Navigator
Sentara Cancer Network

Your Journey beyond

BREAST
CANCER

Tools for the Road

LOUISE B. LUBIN, PHD

YOUR JOURNEY BEYOND BREAST CANCER
TOOLS FOR THE ROAD

iUniverse books may be ordered through booksellers or by contacting:

iUniverse
1663 Liberty Drive
Bloomington, IN 47403
www.iuniverse.com
844-349-9409

ISBN: 978-1-6632-0147-8 (sc)
ISBN: 978-1-6632-0149-2 (hc)
ISBN: 978-1-6632-0148-5 (e)

Library of Congress Control Number: 2021909855

Print information available on the last page.

iUniverse rev. date: 07/15/2021

To Your Health
& Healing
Louise B. Mullin

To the sisterhood of women who
have been my teachers

Preface

In my forty years as a clinical psychologist, I've had the privilege of working with hundreds of women in individual and group settings as they've faced their journey through and beyond breast cancer. They've shared with me their knowledge, pain, and loss as they traveled on this road. Some were recently diagnosed, while others were in active and ongoing treatment, experiencing a reoccurrence, or managing end-of-life decisions. It has been my privilege to walk this journey with all of them. I have gathered over the years these resources and tools that I hope will be useful to you on your personal journey. This guide is not a substitute for professional counseling or medical consultation; rather, it is an interactive manual of important life skills.

We all seek to find wholeness and balance in our lives. Each of you is a unique woman who must find her individual path to healing. When breast cancer challenges you, I hope this guide will help you identify your own road map to move forward. The exercises, activities, and tools provided will increase your knowledge of your body, identify the power of your mind, and connect with the wisdom of your spirit.

I wish to thank my patients, workshop participants, friends, and other health professionals who have given their time, talent, and insights. They have all been my teachers. I also want to thank my husband, Barry, and my family who have always been an optimistic, encouraging force for growth and change.

Thank you for choosing to read this guide. My wish is that it will provide not only useful information and tools but also hope and strength to empower you to move forward on your journey beyond breast cancer.

Introduction

Your doctor just told you that you have cancer. I bet that moment, along with how numb, shocked, and afraid you felt, is frozen in your memory. Your immediate thought might have been, *Am I going to die from this cancer?* After the initial shock and trauma, maybe you thought, *What will I have to go through to try to beat this? How will I ever manage all the physical and emotional changes? How will my family ever deal with this?*

If you are like the many women I have seen as a psychologist over the past forty years, you gathered your resources, educated yourself on what the medical community recommended, and began the difficult first phase of treatment. You counted down your chemo, surgery dates, and radiation sessions and put one foot in front of the other. You pushed through the challenging physical and emotional demands in the hope of reclaiming your life. Your strength has been tested, and you have endured physical pain and many daily challenges. Hopefully the medical community was a source of support and information for you in these initial phases.

After the whirlwind of that first active treatment slows down and your contact with the medical community is less frequent, you probably feel more on your own. You now have the space to question, *What just happened to me? What do I do now?* These questions surface only after enough time has passed and your sense of trauma feels less acute.

In individual as well as group settings, I have been humbled by the resiliency and strength of these women as they faced this life-challenging disease. The word that best describes most of them is *determined*, and their fighting spirit has been a privilege to watch.

You will all be at different points on the time line of treatment. Perhaps you have finished the first phase, are continuing with some additional form of treatment, or are beginning treatment again after a reoccurrence. Because each of you is more than a statistic in a research protocol, your cancer journey will be different from anyone else's. There is no exact right path to follow except the one that is right for you as you attempt to live your own unique life.

At each turn on the road, you will face many hard decisions. You certainly did not choose this challenge, but it is now in front of you. Deciding what is important to you and how you want to live and setting your priorities are some of the demands of this disease.

The challenge is how you want to move forward toward healing. Healing involves taking risks and choosing to take responsibility to find your unique wholeness and balance. The medical community works to achieve a cure, which is the absence of physical disease. Everyone hopes for a cure. Even if you do not achieve a cure, you can and must seek your definition of personal healing.

I have always been fascinated by how the mind, body, and spirit interact to enable healing of disease and illness. I have seen the strength of resolve and change that are possible when a woman commits to identify her needs and learns how to care for her physical, emotional, and spiritual needs. My patients have been my teachers. Many of the life lessons I have learned are included throughout this guide. When you become aware of how precious life is, priorities shift. You can see more clearly the truth of what really matters. You can redefine, rediscover, and reconnect with what is truly important to you.

I have seen how the challenges of cancer continue long after the diagnosis and initial treatment are over. These ongoing life challenges are the basis of this guide. Each chapter will provide you with guidance and information as well as specific tools to address the power of your mind, knowledge of your body, and wisdom of your spirit. You will learn how to physically take care of yourself and make choices each day to practice self-care. You will understand how the power of your thinking is central to your decisions, feelings, and behavior. My focus on spirit is to help you identify and connect to your inner essence, soul, or higher power. Your spirit can also be your sense of being part of a universe greater than yourself. The chapters are as follows:

- Chapter 1, "The Uncertain Roundabout," focuses on how uncertainty and fear of the unknown and possible reoccurrence might cause you anxiety.

- Chapter 2, "The Rough and Lonely Road," describes how cancer is an experience of grief and loss that must be acknowledged and managed.
- Chapter 3, "You Are Not Traveling Alone," discusses cancer as a family affair for not only your immediate family but also significant others in your life.
- Chapter 4, "Focus on the Lane You Are In," provides tools to focus on what you can control: the present moment.
- Chapter 5, "Navigating the Exit Ramp," asks you to face the fear of death that can arise with cancer and how important it is to define your values and needs to others.
- Chapter 6, "Finding Your Path Back Home," directs you to find your way home to the strength and resilience within you.

The road to healing is not one you can travel alone. We all need help whenever we are facing the unknown. Managing the uncertainty of cancer demands that you open yourself up to learning tools and strategies to move forward. There are many paths and roads to healing. The road you take can seem more like a maze than a straight path. There will be times when you hit a roadblock and feel stuck and unable to move forward. Perhaps your treatment is not going well and needs to change or halt for a period of time. You might need to circle back and start again in a different direction. The path might seem narrower when you are feeling alone or wider when you open up to the support from others. Although this guide is not a substitute for either medical or psychological consultation, it is a resource to help you cope and thrive to move forward.

My patients have expressed that cancer has changed their lives in profound ways. Please be aware that the identities and details of the women in the guide have been changed and combined to protect confidentiality. My greatest hope is that what I have learned by traveling with these amazing women will help make your journey more manageable.

This journey is more like a marathon than a sprint. You run a marathon by pacing yourself rather than trying to sprint as fast as you can. This guide should not be read quickly or in one sitting. You might want to have a journal in which to write additional thoughts as they occur to you. As you move through this guide, there will be opportunities to question yourself and commit to take some action. These questions are rest stops to pace yourself as you travel forward. Keep your focus and goals small and specific enough to be able to take a first step. Stretch enough to feel some movement forward, but don't anticipate what might happen and not even begin. The challenges of cancer can reveal to you what is truly meaningful and important in your life. Pay attention not only to what you can change but also to your own inner ability to bring health and healing to your life now and in the future.

> The natural healing force within each one of us
> is the greatest force in getting well.
>
> —Hippocrates

Wherever you are on your journey, I hope you will be able to use these tools and information to move forward to connect with the healing power within you. Let's begin on this journey together.

1

The Uncertain Roundabout

Find Your Route Forward

- Learn how to calm your body.
- Challenge your thoughts to feel more control.
- Face your fears with acceptance and compassion.

How Uncertainty Affects Your Body

Lesson Learned from My Patients

When I can calm my body, I am more able to manage, both physically and emotionally, the challenges of my life.

When you first received your cancer diagnosis, you were thrown into feelings of uncertainty about your future health and well-being. Questions about how, if, and when the cancer might reoccur accompany you long after diagnosis and treatment. Anxiety is always about the future. Your body reacts to your fear of the future as if you were in real physical danger. Your autonomic nervous system is designed to respond and react to real or imagined physical or emotional threat. This system is composed of two parts: the sympathetic (flight, fight, or freeze) and the parasympathetic (rest and digest and relaxation) nervous systems. They affect your body as follows:

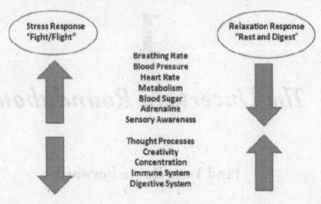

Fight/Flight vs Rest/Digest

Stress Response "Fight/Flight"

Relaxation Response "Rest and Digest"

Breathing Rate
Blood Pressure
Heart Rate
Metabolism
Blood Sugar
Adrenaline
Sensory Awareness

Thought Processes
Creativity
Concentration
Immune System
Digestive System

Where do you feel the effects of stress in your body?

The next time you face some uncertainty, notice how your body reacts. Awareness is the first step to creating change. How does your body react to uncertainty?

Although your sympathetic system can be automatically triggered by many different factors, including heredity, medical conditions, medications, and stressors in your daily life, you do have some control over the parasympathetic (resting) system. One of the ways you can bring about the calming effects of the parasympathetic system is to learn some relaxation tools.

Relaxation is more than just watching TV or taking a bath. Although these activities can be enjoyable, the following tools focus on ways to regularly practice relaxation to bring about a calming of worry and anxiety. How do you slow down your body to feel calmer and safer? The quickest and easiest way to slow down your body and increase your sense of alertness and presence is to adjust your breathing. When you get anxious or fearful, your breath is shallower and more rapid. Try the following to help you relax.

Tool: Abdominal Breathing

1. Focus your attention on your abdomen.
2. Inhale slowly and deeply through your nose.
3. Imagine your chest and abdomen are like a balloon. Fill them with air to allow them to expand.
4. Pause for a moment, and slowly exhale through your nose or mouth. Be sure to exhale slowly and completely, and let your body go.

It is helpful to breathe in on a count of four. Pause and hold your breath for a count of five, and then slowly exhale to a count of seven through your nose or mouth. Try to repeat this for a total of three to five minutes. If you get light-headed, adjust your inhalation, pause, and exhale. Don't push or force your breath, and try to keep your breathing smooth and regular.

I have heard it said there is little difference between how fear and excitement feel in your body. When you are anxious, slowing down your breathing is calming. Making an "Ahh" sound can help you to settle back into your body with more awareness. Plus, it just feels good to exhale some of that tension!

Tool: Mini Relaxations

Adjust your breathing anyplace and anytime. No one needs to know you are doing this. Your breath is with you every moment of every day. Try the following with your eyes open or closed, depending on what you are doing:

1. Count slowly from ten to zero, counting one number on each out breath.
2. While taking a breath, think, *I am*, and on the out breath, think, *At peace*.

3. As you breathe in, count slowly to four, and on the out breath, count back down to one.

4. The next time you face a difficult situation (e.g., going in for a procedure, making a treatment decision, or talking to someone when you feel upset), take three deep breaths before you begin.

The only time these tools won't work is when you don't use them!

Tool: Shifting Your Awareness

1. Close your eyes, and breathe. Notice your body, how the air feels when you breathe in, how your heart beats, and the sensations you have in your stomach and gut.

2. With your eyes still closed, purposefully shift your awareness away from your body to everything you can hear, see, smell, or feel through your skin.

3. Use your senses to shift your awareness outside yourself.

By shifting your awareness back and forth several times between what's going on in your body and what's going on around you, you learn in a physical way that you can control which aspects of your world—internal or external—you notice. You can gain a sense of control over how you react to physical sensations and become better able to manage anxiety. You can grow your ability to observe your thoughts and sensations. In a stressful situation, the goal is to respond, not just react.

Will you try this tool to shift your awareness the next time you feel anxious?

Try doing one of these breathing tools for three to five minutes, and notice if you feel any greater sense of calm in your body. Can you feel your body slowing down? Did your thinking also slow down, or were you focusing on any specific thought or upcoming situation? Did you feel any letting go of tension or tightness in your body or mind?

_____

_____

Carrying Tension in Your Body

Dr. Edmund Jacobson, in the 1930s, developed progressive muscle relaxation. He found that tensing and releasing various muscle groups can increase body awareness and help you create a state of relaxation. A muscle cannot be tense and relaxed at the same time. Knowing the difference between how a tensed muscle feels and how a relaxed muscle feels for you is the aim of this tool. Many of us carry our anxiety and fear in our body when we are stressed. Are you aware if there is a specific place in your body that tenses up when you are stressed? Try the following:

Tool: Jacobson's Relaxation Technique

Find a quiet place where you will not be interrupted. Loosen any tight clothing, take off your shoes, and get comfortable. Give yourself fifteen to twenty minutes at a specific time to try this. Some prefer to do this before they go to sleep.

Don't try too hard. Just let it happen, and don't judge how well you are doing. Keep an open, passive, detached attitude. It does not need to be perfect.

When you tense a particular muscle group, do so with some strength but not strain. Hold it for seven to ten seconds. Concentrate on how the tension feels in your muscles. Release the tension abruptly, and then relax the muscle. Take fifteen to twenty seconds before going on to the next muscle group. You might tell yourself, *I am letting go*, or *I am relaxing*, between each muscle group.

Many people find it helpful to start at the top of the body and work down. Do the following:

- Clench your fists. Hold the tension, and then release.
- Tighten your biceps by bringing your forearms up to your shoulders. Hold the tension, and then release.
- Tighten your triceps (underside of the arm) by extending your arms out straight and locking your elbows. Hold, and then relax.

- Tighten the muscles in your forehead by bringing your eyebrows up as far as you can. Hold, and then release. Feel your forehead go limp.
- Clench your eyes shut tightly. Hold, and relax.
- Open your mouth wide enough to feel your jaw tighten. Hold, relax, and feel your jaw hang loose.
- Tighten the muscles in the back of your neck by pulling your neck back (be careful—not too hard), and hold. Relax, and feel the weight of your head sinking into the surface you are resting on.
- Tighten your shoulders by bringing them up to your ears. Hold, and relax.
- Tighten the muscles around your shoulder blades by trying to get them to touch. Hold, and relax.
- Tighten your stomach muscles by sucking in your stomach. Hold, and relax.
- Tighten your lower back by arching it (use caution if you have any lower back pain). Hold, and relax.
- Tighten your buttocks by pulling them together. Hold, and relax.
- Squeeze your thighs together by tightening your hips along your thighs. Hold, and relax.
- Tighten your calf muscles by pulling your toes toward you. Hold, and release.
- Tighten your toes by curling them downward. Hold, and relax.

Scan your body from head to toe to see if you have any remaining tension. If so, go back to that muscle group, and relax and let go a little more. See a wave of relaxation spread from your head to your toes.

Could you feel any difference in the muscle groups after you tensed and relaxed? It might take some practice before you notice this difference. This tool is useful before bedtime to help you relax to go to sleep.

You might want to have someone guide you through this the first time. Consider buying an audiotape or finding one online. Sounds True and New Harbinger Press are excellent online resources for many other relaxation tools.

Will you give yourself time to practice relaxation to increase your awareness of where and how you hold tension in different parts of your body?

Roadblock: "I Don't Have Time to Relax"

Perhaps you are saying to yourself, "I don't have time to do these relaxation exercises." I know you have many demands on your time and energy. However, I challenge you to think about what is important to you and how you can change the way you manage your time and decide your priorities.

Let's look at why you might feel you have too many pressures to take the time to pay attention to your own special needs. How much do you value yourself? Putting your needs first is not being selfish. Many women have a tough time doing this, as we have been trained to be caregivers and put others first. Although giving to others is a wonderful way to show love and concern, self-care is vital when you are challenged by cancer. Many of my patients put the needs of their children and families before their own physical or emotional needs. They feel guilty about not being able to do what they did before cancer and push themselves to accomplish what feels necessary.

Beth, thirty-four years old, was married to a navy pilot who was deployed for six months, and she had no family living nearby. During her chemotherapy, she struggled to give herself permission to pay a babysitter for her two young children so she could take a nap each day during her treatment. It was a financial decision, but also a choice for self-care. She was able to network and find a teen in the neighborhood, giving herself the break she needed.

Linda, a sixty-year-old office administrator, had a difficult time asking for medical leave when she was beginning a new chemotherapy that caused challenging side effects. She was fearful of being fired but sought out the benefits she was entitled to legally and was able to maintain not only her job but also her health.

Being available for others has been a driving force for my patients, but you cannot make yourself available at the expense of your own well-being. Your illness can and will create change for those who are part of your life. I often say, "If you don't make a deposit in your emotional bank, you won't have any resources to withdraw." Your reading this guide is a good sign that you recognize the importance of how you spend and schedule your precious time. Along with your own beliefs about your own time, others' expectations can stand in the way of your giving yourself the attention and time you need.

I am certain you have many obligations and responsibilities on a daily basis. With the addition of medical appointments, procedures, and perhaps just feeling less physical energy, you can get caught up in feeling time pressure or time urgency. This is the sense that you don't have enough time to do what is needed. This kind of thinking leads to rushing. Rushing can become a bad habit. In addition, in our society, we often value how important someone is by how busy they are. Time is money, and status comes from being too busy.

Time pressure or time urgency can have powerful negative effects on your health. The fight-or-flight response is triggered when you pressure yourself to do more than one thing at a time or feel there is not enough time. Kelly Notaris, in *The Book You Were Born to Write* (2018), says about time, "We never have enough of it, and we think we need a lot of it." A cancer diagnosis might create or increase this sense of urgency when you get caught in the fear of how cancer might change or shorten your life. Do any of us ever feel like there is enough time?

There is real time, and there is the way you perceive time. Time expands or contracts depending on what you are doing or what is happening to you. Waiting for a train to pass can seem to take forever when you are in a hurry to get someplace. However, when you are watching a sunset, time slows in a different way. The way you perceive time is based on what you are doing, your mindset, and your awareness of the experience. Becoming aware of and taking action to manage your time are central to your physical and emotional well-being.

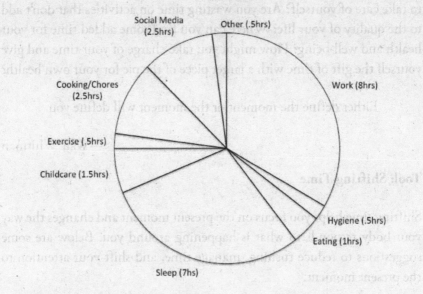

Your Time

Other (.5hrs)
Social Media (2.5hrs)
Work (8hrs)
Cooking/Chores (2.5hrs)
Exercise (.5hrs)
Childcare (1.5hrs)
Hygiene (.5hrs)
Eating (1hrs)
Sleep (7hs)

Consider this time pie an example of how you spend your usual day (if there is ever a usual day!).

Tool: Time Management

Draw a blank circle, and fill in the slices according to how you spend a typical day.

Can you cut the slices in any different way to give yourself more time to take care of yourself? Are you wasting time on activities that don't add to the quality of your life? Where can you find some added time for your health and well-being? How might you take charge of your time and give yourself the gift of time with a larger piece of the pie for your own health?

Either define the moment or the moment will define you.

—Walt Whitman

Tool: Shifting Time

Shifting time helps you focus on the present moment and changes the way your body responds to what is happening around you. Below are some suggestions to reduce rushing, manage time, and shift your attention to the present moment.

- Get to know your body clock. Pay attention to when your peak periods are during the day. Try to identify if you have more attention, clarity, or focus early in the day or later in the evening. Are you a night owl or an early bird?
- Slow down. Don't try to do two things at a time, as rushing leads to poorer results. Discipline yourself to do things more slowly. Eat, walk, and talk more slowly.
- Take brief times off during the day. When you face a delay, look at it as found time. Choose to drive in the right lane instead of the left. You might notice your body feels different in the right lane—probably less tense and strained. When you can't cut back or slow down, vary your rhythm. Always try to take some time out, even if only a few minutes. If possible, alternate when you need to think and when you can move. Change positions often.
- Seek sanctuary from time. Reduce your time on your computer or TV, or try silencing your cell phone or letting it go to voice mail. Consider creating a ritual for either a day or part of a day when you allow yourself enough time to just be and not do. For many religions, this is what the Sabbath, or day of rest, can provide you.

- Learn to schedule. Break tasks into specific steps, and prioritize them. Practice the 25 percent rule: give yourself 25 percent more time to accomplish a task, to allow for interruptions or problems to buffer for success. If you are early, think of the extra minutes as a gift.

- Pay attention to yourself and others to make sure you are on your own calendar. Live according to your own personal standards. Listen to and give attention to the important people in your life. I often have said to patients, "Whose *should* are you listening to? Is it yours or someone else's?" Practice saying no until you get good at it.

How Uncertainty Affects Your Mind

Lesson Learned from My Patients

My life is always changing, despite my desire for it to remain the same. I am often unready for what is taken away or lost or what is going to happen. Although I cannot control what life brings, I can control the way I think about what is happening to me. I am more than my thoughts.

I have found that when you can relax and calm your body, you are more prepared for what is going on in the moment right in front of you. You might find, however, that it is easier to calm your body than your mind. I often describe our minds as being like a puppy: always moving and not easily able to settle down. This is especially true when you feel anxious. We know from understanding the brain that when we are fearful, the part of our brain that helps us focus, the hippocampus, is hijacked by the older part of the brain, the amygdala. This is why it might be hard to think clearly when you are stressed.

Dr. Herbert Benson, in the late 1960s, developed the relaxation response as a Western medical approach to meditation. It is a simple way to relax both your mind and your body by focusing your thoughts on what I call an anchor phrase or word. Imagine your thoughts are like waves in the ocean. Your anchor is what you can always go back to when your mind starts to move in all directions. Below are the instructions.

Tool: The Relaxation Response

1. Pick a focus word or short phrase that's firmly rooted in your belief system, such as *peace, love, one, calm*, or *no problem*.
2. Sit quietly in a comfortable position.
3. Close your eyes. If you wish, you may keep them open.
4. Relax your muscles. Start at your toes, and gradually move up your body to your feet, legs, chest, arms, neck, and face.
5. Breathe slowly and naturally, and as you do, repeat your focus word, phrase, or prayer silently to yourself as you exhale.
6. Assume a passive attitude. Don't worry about how well you're doing. When other thoughts come to your mind, simply say to yourself, "Oh well," and gently return to the repetition.
7. Continue for ten to twenty minutes. (Start with less time if you need to do so.)
8. Do not stand immediately. Continue sitting quietly for a minute before rising.
9. Practice this technique once or twice daily.

Tool: The Relaxing Sigh: "Ahh"

You might catch yourself sighing or yawning during the day. This is your body's way of helping you get more oxygen. A sigh is often felt when things don't feel just right or you feel tension. Sighing can be a way to relax.

1. Sit or stand up straight.
2. Sigh deeply, letting out a sound of deep relief as the air rushes out of your lungs. Try to feel the vibration of the sound move down through your chest.

3. Don't think about inhaling; just let the air come in naturally.
4. Take eight to twelve of these relaxing sighs, and let yourself feel the relaxation.
5. Repeat as you feel the need.

Don't be embarrassed by the sound of your "Ahh!"

Tool: Visualization and Guided Imagery

Visualization involves forming a mental image or picture in your mind. It can help you see in your mind's eye the direction you can go to decrease fear. When people tell me they can't visualize, I say, "Tell me—how many windows are in the front of your house?" Usually, everyone can see this. Try it. I bet you can visualize and count those windows. Although some of you are more visual than others, this tool is another helpful way to relax. Try this:

- Find a comfortable place where you will not be interrupted.
- Imagine yourself in a peaceful place. It might be at the beach, in the mountains, in a cozy chair in front of a fire, or in the forest—wherever you feel safe and relaxed. It might be a place you have been or would like to go.
- Use all your senses. What do you see around you? What smells are there, and what can you hear? There may be silence or not. Is there anything you taste or want to taste? What touch are you experiencing on the surface of your skin—a cool breeze or warmth of the fire? Are you alone or with others?
- Use your imagination to allow this safe healing place to relax you and fill you with peace and calm. Allow yourself to rest in this place for as long as you need. Pay attention to the sense of calm you feel, and know that you can return to this place whenever you need to experience this peace.

You might want to listen to an audio on my website, www. ManyPathstoHealing.com, to hear a guided imagery of a safe healing place.

There are many different types of imagery that patients have found helpful. Some visualize how chemotherapy is shrinking their tumors or how healing light is shining down on them to increase their immune function. Visualization is a personal way to feel more empowered as you move forward on your journey. A wonderful online resource for guided imagery is www.HealthJourneys.com.

Can you think of a situation in which your body needs to be present (e.g., chemotherapy or a medical procedure) but your mind can be somewhere that feels safe and more secure? Consider using visualization during those times to increase your sense of control and strength. In addition, if possible, perhaps listen to some calming music to decrease your stress when you don't have to pay attention to the immediate task or procedure.

Cancer on Your Mind

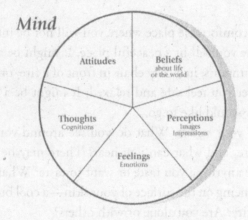

All of the slices of this mind pie affect how you think about cancer and play an important role in your anxiety and fear. Even if you never imagined you could be diagnosed with cancer, you might have had specific thoughts, feelings, perceptions, beliefs, and attitudes about what it would be like to have cancer. All of these aspects of your mind have been influenced by your past experiences as well as your personality. When you feel anxious and fearful, thoughts arise from those feelings.

Our understanding of the physical brain and its role in mental as well as physical health is an exciting frontier for science. Many variables affect your physical brain and play a role in your emotional and physical health, including disease, medication, heredity, environment, sleep, and diet.

Your First Thought about Cancer

You are always thinking. Your thoughts are a continuous stream rather than distinct objects. When you first received your diagnosis, the mental stream went off in a new direction, and the thoughts went to a single preoccupation. The nonstop thought was *cancer*. As time goes by, your thoughts about cancer become more background than foreground. Cancer thoughts do not completely go off the radar screen of your mind. With time and coping tools, cancer thoughts will not be on your mind every minute of each day, as they were when you were first diagnosed. How have your thoughts about cancer changed since your diagnosis? Has the shock moved to determination to manage the physical challenges you might have thought were beyond your control? Although time plays an important role in how you think about your experience with cancer, your specific thoughts strongly influence how you feel as you try to cope.

How many words would it take to say all the ways that going through cancer has touched you? Ernest Hemingway was the first to write a six-word story. Although you could probably write a book, examples of the words women have written are *grateful, isolated, angry, blessed, afraid*, and *loved*.

Tool: Your Six-Word Cancer Journey

What would you say if you had only six words?

_____

_____

Your Beliefs and Perceptions about Cancer

You might not even be aware of the beliefs you had about cancer before you were faced with your diagnosis. Your beliefs are the thoughts you have elevated to the level of truth. They are invisible filters that influence every aspect of your experience and decisions. Many of your beliefs come from your childhood experiences and authority figures. You strongly hold on to them and might have never questioned them at all.

Your perceptions are your beliefs or opinions as to how things seem to you and may be based on your physical senses of what you experience around you.

What are your beliefs about cancer? Doctors? Why you got cancer? What will happen? What about God and spirituality? What about death and life after death? Each of you has unique beliefs that guide your thoughts and behavior. How you create meaning about what has happened to you can be a source of distress or an opportunity to create a sense of hope. My patients who demonstrated the strongest coping skills found their own unique way to make sense of their cancer experiences. For many, providing support and information to other breast cancer patients is part of their healing process.

Do you ever question your beliefs and ask yourself if they are still relevant? Do you seek out information to question the truth of your beliefs?

Your Attitude about Being a Patient

Your attitude includes your feelings and beliefs about being a cancer survivor and influences how you act and behave. Your attitude about being a patient can open you up or shut you down to possibilities and change. If you see yourself as a victim to the disease, you will limit how you approach each challenge. If you exercise the muscle of courage, you will strengthen your fighting spirit, which is the most helpful attitude of survivors. If you focus on what is wrong to the exclusion of what is possible, you affect your healing process by creating hopelessness and more fear.

Your Feelings

When you experience an emotion, your feelings reveal what is going on in your body. Your thoughts continue to give meaning to that emotion. Feelings happen after an emotion and involve thoughts you might not even

16

realize you are having. Feelings are hard to measure precisely. Emotions come and go quickly in your physical body. The thoughts that accompany your emotions will expand or limit how much and how long you feel an emotion. What can determine your life experience is not only cancer but also the meaning and significance you give to cancer.

I have seen women who think about cancer as just a bump in the road they will have to get over to get to the next stop. I will always remember my first breast cancer patient in 1984. Mary, a forty-five-year-old married woman with no children, had already been through multiple experimental treatments to control her metastatic disease. Treatment options were much more limited at that time. I continued to be amazed with her inner strength and determination. She had decided she would run a marathon and did just that. Mary lived another sixteen years with the same attitude of living as fully as she could for as long as she could. As an artist, she created yearly holiday cards that revealed her grit and humor.

However, other women I have worked with have sought to find what they did wrong to cause their cancer, either to correct or to blame themselves. Some see cancer as bad luck and ask, "Why me?" I have worked with women who believe they are being punished for some past behavior and emotionally fold into a victim role. This results in powerlessness and depression. On the other hand, other women approach the *why* question with "Why not me?" Many have no family history and come to realize that breast cancer can affect anyone.

Clearly finding the perspective that helps you manage challenges with as much determination and strength as you can muster is the best route forward.

A take-charge approach is the most beneficial for healing. For example, you might want your chemo given in a different arm. You can assert yourself to the nurse or choose to say nothing and feel powerless and afraid. You might take the risk of asking for more time from your physician even though you know how busy it is in the office. Finding ways to assert yourself in your daily home life is another necessary way to take charge. I have spoken with women who were not supported by family and friends in their decision-making process about specific treatments. They had to go it alone and do what was right for them without the support of those closest to them.

As overwhelming as cancer can be, it does not have to define who you are and what you can achieve in your daily life. Who you are is so much more than a cancer patient. You are more than any disease and more than a statistic. Data from research can provide information, but please always remember you are a *unique* woman. You share many common experiences with your fellow travelers on this road, but your path must be what is best for you.

It is important to realize that all humans are designed and built to worry. We call this the negativity bias. We all tend to remember and focus on negative events rather than positive ones. It has been said that negative events stick like glue, while positive ones are like Teflon. Anticipating what might happen allowed the fittest of our species to survive. Our bodies and brains react to any perceived threat. When you sense that something is wrong, your mind begins searching for what is happening. Physical symptoms, such as pain or discomfort, when the cause is not clear or defined, can often set you on a course of fear. Having a headache after a cancer diagnosis can lead you down the path of assuming the worst and fearing that headache might be another tumor. As important as it is to check out symptoms you are unsure about, it is also valuable to identify how fear is running your thinking.

Whether you realize it or not, you are constantly talking to yourself. Your thoughts lead to feelings that cause you to react in certain ways. Cancer can feel like a loss of control. What is always under your control is the way you think about what is happening to you.

What Is Self-Talk?

- *Self-talk* refers to the running dialogue and thoughts in your mind.
- It is automatic. You don't notice it or the effect it has on you; you just react.
- It appears in shorthand. One short word or image can contain a whole series of thoughts, memories, or associations.
- It always sounds like the truth to you.

It's hard to fight an enemy that has outposts in your head.

—Sally Kempton

Your self-talk can be encouraging or deflating. What you think affects how you feel. When you are in a state of uncertainty and fear, your self-talk focuses on what will happen. The uncertainty of cancer creates thoughts about "what if." In order to focus on what is under your control—the present moment—you must shift gears.

Remember these words:

It's not "what if" but "what now."

Copy this quote, and put it where you can see it often.

When you are worried or fearful and your thinking goes to what might happen, gently tell yourself these words to bring yourself back to what you can manage at that present moment. This is an effective tool you can use anytime and anywhere.

Tool: The STOP Tool

When thoughts arise that cause you to feel fearful or anxious, imagine this stop sign.

- **S: Stop.** As soon as you notice you are feeling anxious, stop what you are doing. Ask yourself: What are your early warning signs? Do you tense up in your body or in your face? Does your breathing change? Do you raise your voice? What exactly do you do? Pay attention when it is happening, and remind yourself, "I must pay attention now."

- **T: Take a Breath.** As you know, when you are emotionally upset, your body and thinking are affected, and your breathing gets shorter. When you slow down your breathing with some abdominal breathing, you have a greater ability to think clearly and use better judgment. You use different parts of your brain when you are calm than when you are fearful. So let yourself exhale, and feel your body relax (like the energy that comes from a sigh). You are then better able to respond rather than react.

- **O: Observe.** With calmer and clearer thinking, you can begin to sort out your feelings. Ask yourself, "What am I telling myself right now? Am I reacting to old patterns? What other choices do I have in this situation? Is there another way to think about this now?"

- **P: Practice Other Choices.** When you are open to change, you can sort out what might be possible. Focus on what might work for you. When you are sorting out a situation, stay away from thinking about what is fair or unfair, is right or wrong, or should or should not be. Try not to evaluate, and try to unglue your opinions. Acknowledge what is happening, but don't judge. Try to meet your needs for this specific situation. Keep the focus on what you can do now.

Think about the last time you needed to do something that was difficult for you. Perhaps you needed a procedure, such as a CAT scan, to evaluate a symptom. Before you even begin the registration process in the office, take a moment to try try this STOP tool. It will help you feel a greater sense of control over what is happening, even if you still need to wait for the results to know what lies ahead in terms of further treatment.

The STOP tool is a helpful way to change the spiral of uncertainty. This tool has been a mainstay of my work with all my patients. You can use it anytime you feel caught up in any situation in which you want to exercise more control and reason before you react without thought or awareness.

Which Voice Is Loudest in Your Head?

With the constant dialogue in your head, there are certain types of personalities that create more anxiety and fear. Which of these describes you best?

- **The Worrier.** Are you the worrier, who anticipates the worst, overestimates the odds of something bad happening, and creates a big image of failure? Does your thinking often go to "what if"

  How about trying to say to yourself, "I can deal with a little anxiety because I know it will pass"? Remember, it's not "what if" but "what now."

- **The Critic.** Are you the critic, who is always judging your and others' behavior? The critic compares you to others, ignores your positive qualities, and leaves you feeling like a failure. She has little self-esteem or self-worth and tells you, "That was stupid. You should be better or stronger." Most of us are our worst critics.

  How about saying to yourself, "I am worthy of the respect of others as well as myself"?

- **The Victim.** Are you the victim, who feels hopeless or helpless? She tells you that you will never feel better, because you are not good enough, and nothing will change. The victim is depressed and uses phrases like "I can't" or "I'll never be able to do that."

  Try telling yourself, "I can continue to make progress one step at a time," or "It is never too late to change."

- **The Perfectionist.** Are you the perfectionist—a close cousin of the critic —who pushes you to do better? You are never good enough. You should be working harder and never make mistakes or have setbacks. "I should," "I have to," and "I must" are her favorite phrases. Question whose *should* you are listening to in your head.

  Try "I don't always have to be ____" or "It's OK to make mistakes." You don't need to be perfect to be worthy of love.

Which of these do you see in yourself? You might identify with more than one. Although you might automatically have these thoughts, you can counter them with more positive, supportive statements. The next time you start down the path of negative self-talk, try to come up with one specific negative thought, and ask yourself these questions:

- Is this thought always true?
- Has this thought been true in the past?
- What are the odds of this being true?

- What is the worst thing that could happen?
- Am I looking at the whole picture?
- Am I being fully objective?

What we think, we become.

—Buddha

Can you identify and write down some of the thoughts that cause you worry and fear? Try asking yourself some of the questions listed above to help yourself feel less anxious and challenge your negative self-talk.

_____

_____

Tool: Shifting Your Thoughts to Reduce Anxiety and Fear

Although your thoughts are automatic and seem to have a life of their own, you can play a role in redirecting or shifting them to reduce your anxiety. Remember, you are more than your thoughts. Try one of these:

- *Use thought replacement.* When you start down the "what if" road, use the STOP tool, and redirect to the present moment. Tell yourself, *It's not "what if" but "what now."*
- *Put worry in a time slot.* Allow yourself a set amount of time to worry, say ten minutes. Stay focused on what you are worried about, and don't become distracted. Start with a specific worry, and when the time is over, it's over. Tell yourself, "I'll worry about this the next time it is scheduled."
- *Put worry away.* Visualize an open container with the top off. See each issue, and put it in the container. You may see the issue as words or give it a shape or symbol that fits for you. Close the container, and put it away on a shelf. You can always go back and pull that container down when you feel better able to do so.

Clearing space can help you focus on the present situation, which is what you can control now.

- *Break the issue into small pieces.* If there is any action you need to take, make a small but clear step to move forward.

Consider if you can set a goal, such as to take some time for self-care, when you are feeling overwhelmed. Perhaps, for example, you can commit to spend ten minutes a day being outside in a quiet space.

If you are too anxious to take any action, remember, your breath is the quickest way to slow down your mind and body. You then might be able to try some of the above tools.

Please remember: *you are more than your thoughts. You can challenge thoughts that cause you stress and anxiety. Although you can't control everything that happens to you, you can control how you think about what is happening to you.*

If you try to have a growth mindset and open yourself up to believing you can change and grow, you will take on more risk and challenges. A fixed, rigid mindset will keep you stuck and feeling more vulnerable. Don't let fear of failure keep you from even trying. I have heard it said that perfectionism is often a cause of procrastination and distress. Don't let trying to be perfect prevent you from even beginning to set a goal.

> Falling down is not failure. Failure comes when
> you stay where you have fallen.

> —Socrates

23

Your Spirit and Uncertainty

Lesson Learned from My Patients

We all fear feeling diminished and vulnerable, which happens with illness. Being able to depend on others requires that I trust them and accept that I can't do it all alone. Acknowledging my vulnerability is the first step in discovering ways to find my power and manage my fear.

I know you remember the moment the doctor said, "You have cancer." You might not remember all the details, but you can physically and emotionally remember how it felt. It was a flashbulb moment. When you experienced this traumatic event, your brain moved into high alert, recorded the event, and caused your body's stress response. This is so common for cancer patients that a term was coined for the anniversary of your cancer: *cancerversary*. You might feel stressed and not even realize when this anniversary occurs. It may be

- the date, month, or time of your diagnosis;
- when treatment ended or is expected to end;
- your surgery date or first biopsy or when the margins were clear; or
- the number of months or years since being told you were cancer free.

It can be any period of time that holds significance to you.

So how do you best manage these emotional reactions? First, be mindful of the calendar. Be on the lookout for the time you associate with the event. It's not that you should be distressed, but knowing that you might feel vulnerable during that time helps you prepare to have a plan to take special care of yourself.

You might think it is better to just try to forget painful times or experiences. The reality is that trying to forget difficult events usually does not work. I once saw this great quote:

> Nothing improves memory more than trying to forget it.
>
> —Author unknown

Tool: Create Your Personal Ritual

Rituals are helpful ways to honor your feelings. *Merriam-Webster's Dictionary* defines a ritual as "a ceremonial act" or "an act or series of acts regularly repeated in a set precise manner." A healing ritual can be anything that reflects and creates value for you. Rituals work best when you believe in their power. Rituals can create a sense of hope and faith. Rituals can be as simple as lighting a candle, taking a pleasurable walk in nature, planting something that will grow, or having a special meal. Whatever it is, it is honoring your experience.

You may want to create a ritual that involves others or just mark your special time by yourself. For many, prayer is a ritual that brings comfort and calm. Use your imagination to create a healing ritual. Honor the importance of your experience, and find a way to mark it that feels nourishing and healing to you. I have had patients create in their homes their own special altars, where they go to find refuge and peace. I have had women manage the loss of their hair by creating a special way and time to cut their hair off with important people in their lives. A wonderful, creative woman used her hair to make a nest for the birds in her yard.

What event on your cancer journey do you want to mark as important and create a ritual to honor its importance to you?

_____

_____

Uncertainty Creates Fear

Fear is part of any cancer diagnosis. What causes you fear might be different from what causes fear in someone else, but your body is designed to react with the fight, flight, or freeze response. You can work to build new patterns both in your brain and in your behavior.

Fear is not a good teacher. The lessons of fear are quickly forgotten.
We are not what we know, but what we are willing to learn.

—Mary Catherine Bateson

Tool: Moving through Fear

F: Face it.
E: Explore it.
A: Accept it.
R: Respond.

Facing your fear is the first step in developing what Tara Brach, PhD calls a *fearless heart*. To begin, you do not have to change your behavior. Just being brave enough to acknowledge that you are afraid is the first step. The energy you use in trying to push your fear away can be redirected toward managing it. Fear is a normal human emotion.

Explore your fear. First, just notice what you are telling yourself about the fear. Identify your self-talk and question it's truth. Consider the possibility that, although your thoughts are certainly real, perhaps they are not true. This questioning can help you find additional ways to think about a fearful situation.

First, go below your neck and into your body to identify what you are feeling in your body. Do you feel tingling? Tightness? Notice your breathing. Slow down your breathing, and try to calm any tension in your body. It may help to imagine a caring friend or loved one and what they might say to you that would be supportive and encouraging (e.g., "I believe in you and your ability to manage this situation").

Clearly, if your fear is too overwhelming and is limiting your daily life, you may want a trained professional to help you manage these feelings to help you move forward. You might just need to step back and accept that you need more time and space to manage the fear. Accept that the sense of vulnerability you feel now does not have to limit your ability to cope in the future. Giving yourself permission to be afraid may be the first step in being able to move forward with less fear.

Next, you must accept your fear. You don't have to like what is causing you to be afraid. Fear is a normal response to uncertainty and the unknown. When you can mindfully face fear so that it is no longer in charge, you bring strength, confidence, and space to your life. You become enlarged and in touch with your goodness, humor, and wisdom. By connecting with your heart and letting yourself be just as you are, you can develop genuine sympathy toward yourself.

Lastly, respond. When you start to feel danger or uncertainty, do the following:

- Use the STOP tool.
- Become aware of your breathing.
- Slow your breathing.
- Place your hand on your heart. The feeling in your body is that you must fix it right now, even if the challenge is external. This moves your focus inward. Placing your hand on your heart is a way to show yourself mindful self-compassion. This act changes the brain's neurons even without your having the answer to your fear. This will help you remember that you can calm anxiety inside yourself even if you do not have all the answers.

Placing your hand on your heart is a way to bring a sense of calm to your nervous system. Stephen Porges, MD, introduced the polyvagal theory (1994), which explains how the vagus nerve and its branches communicate with your brain and regulate your heart, face, breath, and abdominal organs. It explains why you feel calmer and safer when you feel seen or heard by someone you care about. Placing your hand on your heart is a way to engage, connect, and calm yourself.

This tool will help your body produce tend-and-befriend hormone. It is the antidote to the hormone adrenaline, which is produced when you are stressed.

Will you place your hand on your heart now, breathe deeply, and allow an image of loving peace to emerge? Perhaps it is the love you feel toward another or someone who loves you deeply. Can you notice any shift in how you feel?

Traveling Forward on the Uncertain Roundabout

As you prepare to leave the Uncertain Roundabout and move further in this guidebook, you continue to be reminded that cancer brings change and uncertainty. Despite all your efforts to try to keep your life steady and under your control, nothing is constant but change. When the unexpected occurs, you want to try to make sense of it. When you can't understand what has occurred, you may feel fear and anxiety.

Focusing on what you *can* control and what you *can* change can bring hope and increased well-being. When you try to do anything you believe is healthy and healing, you not only change the way you feel emotionally but also change your brain chemistry. Although you can't alter everything you want, you can explore what you can change and feel less a victim to cancer. Remember that no matter what is happening to you, what you tell yourself inside your head is always under your control.

The uncertainty of cancer shines a light on the impermanence of your life. Some say this impermanence is what makes a situation holy. You might choose to go to the ocean to experience the vast horizon and see the ongoing movement of the waves to help calm yourself. Just like the ocean, nothing stays the same, as much as we want it to. Change is hard, but when it is necessary, will you fight the waves or learn to swim with the tides back to shore? I hope some of these tools will help you begin to navigate this road of uncertainty. Will you commit to some change?

Change is never easy. To move forward, goals need to be specific, realistic, and not too demanding. You should be able to measure your progress. It also helps to write your goals down and set a date to begin. To benefit from the information and tools in this chapter, I ask you to set at least one goal to address each of the three components of body, mind, and spirit. Below is a sample contract you can modify to work just for you. I have included examples in parentheses.

Committed Action Contract

To manage stress and tension in my body, _____

(I will practice progressive relaxation for two weeks once a day.)

To worry less, _____

(I will use the STOP tool when I am faced with a challenging medical or interpersonal situation in the next week.)

To nourish my spirit,_____

(I will find at least fifteen minutes a day to schedule time to bring myself comfort and inner peace.)

I will begin these changes by _____(specific date).

With a body that is calm and centered, a mind that is aware, and an acceptance that fear may at times accompany you, your committed action will help you find your way forward on the Uncertain Roundabout.

2

The Rough and Lonely Road

Shine Light Where There Is Darkness

- Discover the tools to nurture your body.
- Challenge the thoughts that keep you stuck.
- Let go of blame, and build your hope muscle.

I t can't be denied: cancer is a major loss. You might feel your body has
betrayed you and ask yourself, "Why has this happened to me?" You
might decide that the *why* questions are too difficult and that you can
deal only with the *how*: "How will I move forward when I have so much
to manage?"

Your body has endured many challenging procedures and changes.
You have most likely experienced pain and discomfort. You know your
body has been through a major change. Depending on where you are in
your cancer journey, your body, mind, and spirit have been challenged,
poked, prodded, and stuck more times than you would wish on your worst
enemy. You are aware of not only the loss of health and perhaps your breast
but also the challenge of letting go of what your life was before cancer.
Somehow, you will try to move toward a new way of functioning while
the needle of normalcy is constantly changing. What is this so-called new
normal everyone talks about? However you try to define *normal*, it will be
as unique and individual as each of you.

In this chapter, we will look at how you can honor and respect your
body through sleep, movement, nutrition, and laughter. We will discuss

how you can identify your self-talk to manage with more strength. We will also explore what helps nurture your spirit so you can soothe yourself and your wounds. Cancer can be a traumatic event for some, yet for others, it is just a difficult detour. Each woman I have known has brought her own attitude and perspective to how she views these losses. No matter how much sadness, anger, or guilt you feel, hopefully these tools will help you find a better balance. As this guide is not a substitute for professional help, I will provide you with ways to evaluate what you might need if you seek professional care on your journey.

It is impossible to present a picture that everything is OK, as much as everyone in your world would like it to be. You will need more time to emotionally manage your grief than those around you might think is reasonable. They want you to be positive because they struggle with how to help when they are not able to fix it for you.

I have seen this play out particularly with men who are into doing and fixing things for their spouses. Feeling powerless to fix your breast cancer, many partners may get frustrated and either withdraw or get angry. I have seen some relationships fall apart with the stress of cancer, and I also have witnessed amazing growth and connection between partners going through the journey as a team. As the process evolves for you, many of the relationships in your life will also change and evolve. It is normal to grieve when you lose anyone or anything you love or value.

Being able to share the loss with those closest to you is challenging but necessary for healing. Whether it is an intimate partner, family member, or friend, you must have a safe space to share your fears and sense of loss. Our society has a difficult time with grief and views it as an affliction that must be erased. We must recognize that grief is on a continuum of emotions. Grief leads to sadness, which can lead to clinical depression. Grief is, however, part of the human condition. You must give yourself time to experience your loss and grief.

Feeling sorrow and distress can lead to a sense of sadness. Sadness is not the same as clinical depression, which interferes with your ability to function in your daily life. We will explore and define depression, which is a psychological as well as physical imbalance. It is also not unusual to feel anger when you go through any loss. How you manage your anger plays a role in how you will move forward. Staying angry has been described as swallowing poison and waiting for the other person to die. If you direct your anger at yourself, you will probably become depressed. Anger can be viewed as energy. How you direct this energy is important for your healing.

For every minute you are angry, you lose sixty seconds of happiness.

—Ralph Waldo Emerson

Let's begin to walk the difficult path of loss to help you discover more solid ground with a greater sense of meaning and purpose.

Tending Your Body on the Lonely Route

> **Lesson Learned from My Patients**
>
> Each of us is a unique individual and not a statistic. Identifying what is needed to support my body toward healing is my responsibility. My body will just scream louder at me if I do not listen to it and find ways to take care of and nurture it.

How Do You Know If You Are Depressed?

Depression is a physical as well as psychological condition. There are many causes for depression. Cancer treatment, surgery, medication, prolonged stress, and loss can all create symptoms of depression. How you feel or express loss or grief is unique to you. On this continuum of grief, sadness, and depression, there are some general markers.

When you are sad,

- you still feel connected to others,
- you know that your sadness will end,
- you are still able to enjoy pleasant memories,
- you feel self-worth,
- your sadness comes in waves,
- you can feel pleasure and look forward to the future, and
- you want to live.

For example, many women have had to manage the disappointment of being unable to attend an important occasion because they were too weak and immune compromised to be in a crowd. They were saddened by this loss but able to accept their limits and do what was best for their health at that time. Others have expressed sadness at the changes in friendships when others disappointed them or withdrew from them during their cancer journey. Sadness is painful but does not prevent you from finding the light and joy still present in your life.

When you are depressed,

- you feel alone and outcast,
- you believe that sadness is permanent,
- you feel regret and think about it often,
- you put yourself down and feel critical and negative,
- you believe your sadness will be constant and ongoing,
- you feel no hope or interest in the future,
- you enjoy few activities, and
- you might have thoughts about self-harm.

For example, some of the women I see in individual therapy are struggling with feelings of depression that are affecting their ability to manage their daily lives. They are not able to sleep, lack energy, and have little appetite even after their chemotherapy is completed. They isolate themselves from family and friends and are unable to see that the future can be different from the dark present. The cause of their grief is as individual as each of them. It might focus on the loss of a breast, their inability to have children, physical changes due to menopause, or how cancer has caused them to have to change or leave a job they loved. They feel hopeless and helpless and cannot see the light beyond the dark clouds of their depression.

Some common signs and symptoms of depression are as follows:

SIGNS AND SYMPTOMS OF DEPRESSION

Difficulty sleeping or sleeping too much
Difficulty concentrating
Feeling of hopelessness or helplessness
Overwhelming and uncontrollable negative thoughts
Loss of appetite or significant increase in appetite
Increase in irritability, aggression or anger
Increase in alcohol consumption and/or reckless behavior
Thoughts that your life is not worth living

SADNESS ---DEPRESSION

It is important to remember that not all cancer patients get depressed. In fact, most do not experience many of the symptoms listed in the above chart. Sometimes it is difficult to evaluate if you are depressed, as a serious illness, such as cancer, and its treatment can produce many of the same physical symptoms (e.g., weight loss, sleep disturbance, and loss of energy).

Clearly, you may be experiencing some of these symptoms. Grief decreases over time and occurs in waves, while a more serious depression is persistent and ongoing. If you are experiencing five or more of the above symptoms daily and they continue for more than two weeks, talk to your physician to evaluate if you need medication or counseling.

In my practice, I have seen many women who never had problems with depression prior to their cancer. After treatment, they struggled with symptoms of depression and felt that medication for depression or anxiety was helpful in their ability to cope. Many of them struggled with the idea of taking one more pill. It is a fact that all medications have side effects. Chemotherapy can create a biological imbalance that affects the functioning of your brain. Chemotherapy is a mind-and-body experience. I have often said, "Chemotherapy doesn't affect you only from the neck down." The mind and body work together. Taking medication to balance the effects of other medications is not easy to accept, but it is a reality for some. As much as I believe that medication for depression and anxiety is not the only answer, it is often a missing part of the puzzle when you are clinically depressed. Please remember that depression is not a sign of weakness and is a treatable condition. Don't hesitate to seek out the support you need.

For some, support groups are a safe place to share your feelings, but you may want your own individual counseling to talk through what you are feeling and find specific tools that will help you.

Finding a Therapist

Your local mental health association, local psychologists, or licensed clinical social workers can offer counseling options in all communities. Online, the *Psychology Today* Therapy Directory and the National Register of Health Service Psychologists (www.findapsychologist.org) are excellent resources. You may need to contact your insurance company to check out which providers are in your insurance network. You might want to check out the theoretical orientation of a therapist:

- Psychodynamic focus is on the unconscious motivations of your behavior.
- Solution-oriented or behavioral focus is on the here and now.
- Cognitive behavioral focus is on your thoughts and how to challenge them.
- Family systems focus looks at your family and how each member plays a role in affecting the others.

Many therapists describe their approach as eclectic, which means they use more than one theoretical approach. You clearly want someone who is licensed in the state in which you live. People often wonder about the different types of therapists. Licensed social workers and professional counselors generally have a master's degree. Licensed clinical psychologists have a doctoral degree in psychology. Today, in general, most psychiatrists tend to focus on medication evaluation and do not conduct much therapy.

Although it is helpful to work with a therapist who has experience in working with cancer patients, most qualified therapists are skilled in working with loss and the impact of illness. Many primary care physicians and oncologists are willing to prescribe medication for depression, but they might also want you to see a therapist who can provide you with a broader understanding of your feelings as well as tools to cope. You should give yourself enough time to get to know a therapist to see how you relate to that person. The relationship with your therapist is central to your moving forward. You need to feel heard, safe, and supported. You will not always leave a session feeling better, especially if you are dealing with difficult issues. However, you need to feel that you are being given tools to cope and manage more effectively. You may want to work with a therapist for more than one session before you decide whether to continue to meet for other sessions. Building a relationship can take more than one session.

Joining a Support Group

When I first began working with breast cancer patients, I thought everyone should join a support group. My views have changed over the last four decades. Some of my patients have a level of support from family and friends that provides them what they need to manage the challenges. For others, individual or family counseling is the best use of their time and energy. Overall, it is vital to have someone you trust with whom you feel safe in sharing your hopes, fears, and complaints. We all need to find someone who can listen without judging when we are going through difficult times.

Ideally, a support group of other women who have direct knowledge of your journey is a source of empowerment and solidarity. Professionals lead some groups, and others are peer led by other survivors. Most of the groups are open to new members and include women who are in different stages in their cancer journey. Women who are further along can offer helpful input and information. At the same time, it is important to remember that you are unique, and your body and treatment must be tailored to your needs.

In any group, you must be prepared to encounter women who

experience reoccurrences and eventually lose their lives to cancer. You must recognize that sharing your grief with others can be supportive but also create some anxiety in you. The connection, love, and joy you receive from other women can help you emotionally in facing your fears.

I recognize that many women are not looking for the support of other women but find their support in other ways. Each of you needs some source of caring concern from people who matter to you. Some women find that an online group works better for them. Others are just looking for information about how to make better decisions about treatment. I have also found that the needs of each woman will change as she progresses along her road after diagnosis. When you first get diagnosed, you want information. As you move along, what you need from other patients will change as your life and treatment evolve. Try to identify what you need from other survivors, and let that guide your decision about participating in a support group.

The strength of a group of women who are dedicated to each other and to the cause of emotional and physical healing can be a powerful force for change. Having spoken to many different groups of women over almost forty years, I know that support groups are a vital part of the healing journey for many. I have experienced with them the feelings of connection and empowerment that come from being with others who know in a powerful way the challenges of managing cancer. Others who have walked the walk have a perspective that can feel safe and allow you to feel heard. Being with other women joining together for the collective good is a powerful force for change no matter the common cause.

I saw this power in 2006 when I presented at a breast cancer retreat. Mary Beth, a young survivor, met René, another survivor who was volunteering at the retreat for the hospital system as the good-health fairy. René, dressed in a fairy dress and tennis shoes, connected with the energy and motivation of Mary Beth. Together they understood that there were unique needs for young women (diagnosed before fifty-one years old) that were not being met in their community. They began to gather with other survivors and share information and mutual concerns. They founded the nonprofit Beyond Boobs as a model for providing peer-led support in members' homes. They created a community providing weekend retreats, educational programming, a calendar, and amazing activities and opportunities to belong and share. They expanded in 2015 and are now called Here for the Girls (H4TG). Their sisterhood has expanded to other states as they continue to empower their members. Whether you are able to give to others or perhaps only able to receive at this point in your journey, being part of such a community can bring healing.

Improving Your Quality of Life to Reduce Depression

Cancer is a powerful physical challenge. Although I am not a physician, I can offer you some specific tools to improve the physical quality of your life. Surgeries, radiation, and medication all affect not only your body but also your emotional state. Below are some behaviors that can help you feel stronger during your journey and reduce the impact of cancer on your body and mind.

The Importance of Sleep

I am sure you realize that sleep is a vital part of any healing process. Sleep helps repair your body but also helps improve memory and concentration, which can be affected by chemotherapy. I probably don't need to tell you that chemo brain is real. Menopausal symptoms can also affect your sleep. You might have difficulty either falling asleep or staying asleep or both. These tools may improve the quantity and quality of your sleep, but you may also need medication from your doctor if you don't see improvement. There are many choices, but consulting your doctor is vital. Even if you are taking herbal supplements, your medical doctor must be informed. Be sure to ask your doctor if any of the medications or chemotherapy you are taking might be affecting your sleep.

Tool: Improve Your Sleep

Your Bedroom

- Remove cell phones and laptops.
- Make sure the temperature is right and the room is dark.

- Put alarm clocks out of sight.

Sleep Hygiene

- Commit to a regular bedtime and awakening time.
- Do a relaxing bedtime ritual.
- Reduce caffeine and chocolate after midafternoon.
- Reduce alcohol, as it causes sleep to be fragmented.
- Avoid emotional conversations before bedtime.
- Avoid vigorous exercise in the evenings.
- Use your bed only for sleeping and sexual activity.

Challenge Your Worry about Sleep

Worrying about not being able to sleep can create more sleep problems. If you can't fall sleep after fifteen to twenty minutes, get up and do something that is relaxing until you get sleepy, and then go back to bed. Be aware of keeping the lights low. Consider listening to music, doing guided imagery, journaling, or doing another activity that soothes you.

Try asking yourself, "What is the worst thing that might happen if I am tired tomorrow?" Most of us create a catastrophe in our minds when we can't go to sleep. You might not be your best, but you will be able to function, even if you are not at 100 percent. As simple as this sounds, I often tell patients not to look at the clock when they get up. Looking at the clock will only lead to worry that you are not asleep. Turn the clock or alarm around, and don't look!

Naps often get a bad rap. Napping is respectable and should be guilt free. A brief nap can revive the brain and should be no longer than thirty minutes scheduled midday so as not to disturb your biological clock. Try to keep your nap at the same time each day if possible. Give yourself the gift of a nap if you need one!

You Have to Move

Cancer fatigue is clearly a factor in how you feel both physically and emotionally. Emotional stress along with treatment effects can push you down physically. One of the ways trauma can affect your body is to create a sense of feeling frozen. The idea of movement can be seen as a metaphor. Being stuck is a feeling that can apply to both your emotional state and your physical state. It goes without saying that you should check with your physician regarding which options are right for your physical activity.

Cancer-related fatigue can often be reduced by moderate exercise, which can increase your muscle strength, joint flexibility, and cardiovascular functioning; protect bones; and help control weight. An exercise program should include:

- moderate aerobic workout that pumps up your heartbeat, such as brisk walking, swimming, cycling, or running, for at least 150 minutes per week (per the recommendation of the American Cancer Society);
- strength training to build bone and muscle mass (including tendons and ligaments);
- stretching to increase range of motions and muscle elasticity, improve circulation, and help in body repair to keep joints and muscles limber; and
- balance training to help those with less bone mass regain mobility and strength and prevent dangerous falls and broken bones.

Exercise affects your brain chemistry. It elevates mood and helps reduce feelings of depression. Any positive change you feel when you first try to move might be subtle, but it's worth at least trying. Some helpful tips are as follows:

- Find something you enjoy doing either alone or with a friend.
- Find daily opportunities to move, such as gardening, housecleaning, or walking the dog.
- How about putting on some music and dancing?

Finding an exercise program for cancer patients is a great option. If you can't find one, seek out a professional, and modify an exercise program as needed with them.

As far as finding a way to move that is healing, I strongly suggest you consider yoga as a wonderful way to move, stretch, and reconnect with your body. Yoga is a lot more than just exercise. This ancient discipline can help you disconnect from external stimulation and connect with your inner body and mind. Setting aside time to do yoga is healing. There are even chair yoga and restorative yoga classes that adapt to many physical limitations. This practice is an ideal bridge between mind, body, and spirit. Offering yoga at cancer retreats clearly showed me how powerful an experience it was for all who attended. Whether you are able to do each pose or not does not matter. With a trained instructor, you can find ways to connect and build more awareness and compassion with your body. Learning to befriend your body is a first step in finding more balance and healing. Give yourself the time and space to get on the yoga mat.

Can you make a commitment to yourself to make one small change in how you physically move to increase your vitality? Think of it as moving forward rather than exercise.

_____

_____

Nutrition for Your Mind and Body

Food not only fuels your body but also plays an important role in how you feel emotionally. Educating yourself on how nutrition helps to maintain good physical and psychological health is part of improving the quality of your life. I have included a checklist from Dr. Leslie Korn for you to begin to learn how the food you eat affects your mood, energy, and body. Consider using this chart for three days to familiarize yourself with this important information.

Tool: Food-Mood Diary

Food-Mood Diary and Clinician Checklist

Food-Mood Diary

Name: _____ Date: (dd/mm/yy)_____

Write down everything you eat and drink for three days, including all snacks, beverages, and water. Please include approximate amounts. Describe energy, mood or digestive responses associated with a meal/snack, and record it in the right-hand column. Use an up arrow (↑) for an increase in energy/mood, down arrow (↓) for a decrease in energy/mood, and an equal sign (=) if energy/mood is unchanged.

Time of waking:_____ a.m. / p.m.

Meal	Beverages	Energy Level (↑, ↓, or =)	Mood (↑, ↓, or =)	Digestive Response (gas, bloating, gurgling, elimination, etc.)
Breakfast (Time:_____)				
Snacks (Time:_____)				
Lunch (Time:_____)				
Snacks (Time:_____)				
Dinner (Time:_____)				
Snacks (Time:_____)				

Copyright, Leslie Korn. 2015 Nutrition Essentials for Mental Health (Norton, 2015).

Tool: Food-Mood Checklist

This chart has some specific goals that Dr. Korn recommends for maintaining good physical and emotional health. What, how, and when you eat are all part of good nutrition. Can you find some small way to improve your nutrition?

Clinician Checklist for the Food-Mood Diary

Question	Answer	Goals and Recommendations
1. How much time passed between when the client awakens and when they eat breakfast? Is the client eating breakfast?		One should always eat breakfast, containing at least 3–4 ounces of protein within 30 min-utes of waking for proper energy and blood sugar balancing.
2. How much water/broth is the client drinking throughout the day?		Water intake should be about 50 percent of body weight every day in ounces (example: if a person weighs 160 lb, they should be drinking 80 ounces of water daily).
3. How often is the client eating? How many hours between each meal or snack?		Food should be eaten every 3–4 hours to prevent mood swings, and the client should have at least 3 meals/day and 2 snacks.
4. How many servings of vegetables is the client eating per day?		At least 3 servings of vegetables should be eaten every day. A serving equals from ½ to 1 cup.
5. Is the client eating raw vegetables and fruits?		At least 1–3 servings of raw fruit or vegetables should be eaten every day.
6. Is the client eating enough protein? Note if lack of protein corresponds to drops in mood.		Proteins help to stabilize energy and balance mood and should be emphasized during the daytime hours.
7. Is the client eating enough fats? Note if lack of fats corresponds to mood shifts.		Fats help to stabilize energy and balance mood and should be emphasized during the daytime hours.
8. How many servings of starchy carbohy-drates is the client eating and at what times of day?		During the day carbohydrates are best when combined with protein, and carbohydrates should be emphasized in the evening for relaxation.
9. What is the quality of the food the client is eating (freshly prepared vs. canned or prepackaged foods)?		Recommend whole, fresh, organic foods over packaged and canned foods.
10. Is the client eating enough soluble fiber?		Soluble fiber is found in foods like oat bran, nuts, beans, lentils, psyllium husk, peas, chia seeds, barley, and some fruits and vegetables. Men should be eating about 38 grams/day, and women 25 grams/day.
11. Is the client eating enough insoluble fiber?		Insoluble fiber is found in wheat bran, corn, whole grains, oat bran, seeds and nuts, brown rice, flaxseed, and the skins of many fruits and vegetables.

Given my limited training in the science of nutrition, I will not attempt to suggest which specific foods you should or should not eat to help heal your body. However, as far as the important attitudes for healthy eating, I do have some suggestions.

1. Your body should be viewed with care and love. Treat it as a valued temple that has endured a lot of struggle to find a new balance.
2. Try to recognize when you are physically hungry and need to eat. What do you really want in that present moment? We all eat for

many reasons other than physical hunger. We eat when we are sad, bored, and happy as well as to interact with others.

3. Remember that your body needs good fuel to help you manage the effects of treatment. Even if you don't feel hunger, be sure to nourish your body in small, frequent portions to provide it care and concern.

I have seen how body image can change after cancer. Your body image is the way you think about your appearance and how attractive you are to others. Many women tell me they don't want to "look like a cancer patient" and feel unattractive with all the changes to their body shape and size. Finding nourishing and healthy ways to treat your body is the first step in finding some peace with how you look. The goal is to feel strong and healthy, not to try to achieve some societal view of how you should look. Of course you want to feel attractive. When you truly value yourself, you have the motivation to seek out ways to modify the impact of cancer on your body. You will look different, but *different* does not have to feel *less than*. I have seen how gaining self-esteem and valuing themselves has enabled women to hold their bodies differently and look others in the eye for the first time. Changing your posture can increase your sense of strength. (Just notice how you are holding your shoulders.) Take charge of how much power you give to others' expectations of how beauty and attractiveness should look. Create your new you with a goal of vitality and physical strength. Valuing yourself can direct the choices you make for your self-care.

The Role of Light

Light plays an important role in your mood. Sixty percent of people with depression are subject to seasonal affective disorder (SAD). In the *Diagnostic and Statistical Manual (DSM-5)* published by the American Psychiatric Association, SAD is a type of depressive disorder affected by seasonal shifts in light and the timing of light. It often affects people around Thanksgiving to Easter. Light goes from your eye to your pineal gland, which affects melatonin. This hormone affects sleep, your circadian rhythm, and sleep cycles. Try to get natural sunlight during those cold dark months, but also check out a light box with a brightness of 10,000 lux. Be sure to check with your doctor to make sure this is a good choice for you. Remember, being outside when you can is another way to expose yourself to the benefits of light. Even a short walk around the block can be helpful to change your energy and mood. Consider finding a spot in your house where the natural light comes through. How about creating a special space for yourself to sit and enjoy that light when you can?

The Role of Laughter

A cheerful heart is good medicine.

—King Solomon

When you feel unhappy, laughter seems unlikely. However, it may be some of the best medicine. Research shows laughter can stimulate your immune system by lowering cortisol and can function as a form of exercise. It increases your heart rate and blood pressure. When you laugh, oxygen surges through your body, and your body releases endorphins (the natural high), which can decrease stress. An online resource (www. laughteronlineuniversity.com) provides many examples of how laughter can reduce pain and stress. Laughter is like an internal jogging that affects the body and can reduce anger. When we laugh with others, we create a connection and sense of shared humanity.

Laughter is not a tough pill to swallow!

Laughing is the sensation of feeling good all over
and showing it principally in one spot.

—Josh Billings

What makes you laugh? Find funny videos, and pay attention to the joy and humor in simple situations during your day.

On YouTube, check out Loretta La Roche, a medical humorist whose passion for joy is infectious. I have shown her videos many times and laugh each time even more than I did before.

As you look back on this section regarding how your body reacts to treatment, what is one behavior you can focus on to create more energy and vitality? Start with one small, specific change you can begin in the next few days. Make it a small step that you can build on. Focus on how this step can build your sense of well-being and personal power. Commit to make it happen!

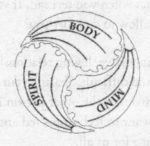

Your Mind on the Lonely Route

> **Lesson Learned from My Patients**
> My thoughts are my reality, although I must challenge and examine them to better manage my reactions and decisions. I can identify possibilities when I challenge my negative, limiting thoughts. I am more than my thoughts.

Cancer is a major stressor that can create a swirl of emotions that are difficult to name, identify, or even understand. Many of us have a difficult time in finding the words or labels to use to describe our feelings. Do you say, for example, "I am angry," when you are really fearful or hurt? Catch the emotion when it happens, and try to name it. Here are some helpful ways to understand your feelings of sadness more clearly.

Tool: Understanding Your Sadness

1. Try to sort out how the emotion of sadness feels in your body. Does your stomach tighten or your breath change? Do you clench your fist or tighten your jaw? This might be hard to notice at first, but keep trying.
2. What was the trigger or prompting event that caused your sadness?
3. What is the self-talk in your head? Are you telling yourself, "I just can't handle this"?
4. Pay attention to how you feel and think about what you need or don't need to do when you feel sadness. Do you feel you must be alone or reach out to others? Perhaps there is a more constructive, healing way to act when you feel sad. If you feel you need others, whom will you allow to comfort you?

I have seen how a supportive, loving relationship can help the road to healing seem less lonely and difficult. Sharing your fears and needs requires that you feel safe and trust that the other person is with you emotionally because they care. You want to feel supported and not pitied. Facing our vulnerability is a challenge for us all.

Remember, sadness can lead to other emotions, such as anger, fear, and negativity. Emotions rise and fall with your self-talk and thinking. Sadness can become a mood and overtake your personality or affect who you really are. Emotions move quickly. Your thoughts play a major role in your keeping your sadness going or trying to move beyond it. Continuing to replay events and think about what has happened will keep you stuck emotionally. You cannot prevent or control what will happen.

You do have control over *what you think* about the things that have happened to you and *how you react* to those events.

Anger and Your Body

Although anger is a normal response to stress and loss, it is not healthy for your body when anger is prolonged and constant. Often, underneath anger is fear that is not always easily identified. Anger causes your brain to release the stress hormones cortisol and adrenaline, which affect your memory and judgment. Anger also decreases your serotonin, the chemical in your brain that helps you feel happier and more positive. Anger can affect your digestive system, slow your metabolism, increase blood pressure and heart rate, and decrease your body's immune system. Although you might not be able to stop your anger from bubbling up, you can find ways to moderate it and not allow anger to control your behavior and health.

What is one behavior you can use to calm your body and mind when you feel anger is running your mind and affecting your body? (Look back at chapter 1 for some tools for reducing that feeling of arousal, whether it is anxiety or anger.)

_____

_____

Tool: Get Unhooked

Below is a helpful tool that focuses on how you think about what is happening to you. I have used this in my practice for many years. Try to imagine that you are a fish swimming through the water of your day. There might be many situations that cause you to feel annoyed or upset. If you think about such a situation as a hook, you can choose not to grab that hook and instead to pass it by.

Think of a situation that occurred today that might have felt like a possible hook. Perhaps someone forgot an appointment with you or was rude or impolite. Take charge of how you want to swim through your day! You don't need to get caught up in every possible hook. Certainly, some annoying events need attention, but more than likely, there are many other situations you can just pass by as you keep swimming forward. Be like that fish: notice the hook for what it is, and choose to pass it by and swim forward.

GET UNHOOKED FROM FRUSTRATION

Negative Self-Talk

You might not realize it, but you are talking to yourself all the time. Although your thoughts are automatic and involuntary, how you choose to react and respond to them is up to you. Stinking thinking involves falling into traps that limit your perspective and ability to respond in healthier ways. Some examples of these common thinking distortions are as follows:

- **Black-and-White Thinking.** The words *never* and *always* are the key words to challenge with this kind of thinking. It is all-or-nothing thinking, such as *I will never feel better, I always am being challenged,* or *I did this wrong, so I must be a real loser.*
- **Tunnel Vision.** Are you seeing only the negative aspects of a situation, a person, or yourself? What other information do you ignore to select only what proves your point? Is your view only the half empty versus the half full?
- **Negative Interpretation.** How much do you mind read and assume without asking what someone else is thinking? Do you think you know without external proof why people act the way they do toward you? You can only know for sure what others are thinking or feeling if you ask or they tell you. Then you must believe they are being honest with you.

- **Personalization.** Do you assume everything others say or do is a reaction to you? Do you blame yourself for things that are not your fault and take responsibility for events beyond your control? Might there be others things going on that are not about you?
- **Being Right.** How often do you try to prove you are right and others are wrong? Do you expect others will change their point of view if you just make your point strongly enough?

Think of a time that caused you to struggle with a person or a particular situation. Try to identify what you are telling yourself about this. Consider how you can try to come up with an authentic, accurate alternative to these distorted thinking patterns.

Challenge your stinking thinking so your world can smell better!

Tool: Challenge Your Thinking

My negative thought is

_____

_____

I will ask myself the following:

- Does this thought contribute to my stress?
- Where did I learn this thought?
- Is this thought logical?
- Is this thought always true?

A more accurate, authentic alternative thought is

_____

_____

As we talk about assumptions you make, I think it is important to challenge some of the inaccurate assumptions that others make about cancer patients.

- **Assumption 1:** When active treatment is over, things will get back to how they were before cancer. Although healing from cancer is a process, the awareness of vulnerability and mortality changes, as well as priorities and beliefs about what is important. Life can resume much as before, but the lens and filters are different.

- **Assumption 2:** Having the doctor say, "There is no sign of cancer on your tests," allows you to feel there is no need to worry. The fear that cancer will return is present in your life for an extended period of time. Learning to live with this uncertainty is one of the greatest challenges of this disease. Finding the tools to tame the dragon of fear and challenge the "what if" thinking takes effort and commitment from you.

- **Assumption 3:** All cancer patients become depressed. Being sad or worried is not clinical depression. Knowing when and if you need help is based on identifying your symptoms and responses to your daily life.

- **Assumption 4:** Cancer patients need everyone around them to always be hopeful and optimistic. For sure, we all need hope. What you hope for must change as your circumstances change. Realistic optimism is much preferred to being told, "There is no need to worry."

- **Assumption 5:** Death is failure. We all struggle with loss and don't want to leave those we love. It is important to realize there might be a time in every person's life when they want to stop active treatment without being seen as a quitter. You have the right to choose how you want to manage your cancer journey.

The Optimist-Pessimist Balance Bar

As I mentioned before, your thinking might cause you to view your glass as half empty or half full. Look at this scale, and evaluate your thoughts about your cancer experience.

Rate each statement from 1 to 5, and calculate the total. Where are you on this scale? The higher your total, the more you tend to be pessimistic in your thinking about your cancer journey.

Expect a more positive future	Expect a more negative future
1------------------------ 2------------3------------------------4--------------5	
When negative things happen, believe it will change	Generalize events as going to stay the same
1--------------2----------------------- 3------------------------4--------------5	
Distract yourself when difficult events happen	Blame yourself when difficult events happen
1--------------2-----------------------------3------------------------4--------------5	
Believe you are better than most at managing challenges	Believe you are less able than most at managing challenges
1--------------2----------------------- 3------------------ 4------------------5	
Think, *It could be worse*	Think, *It will not get better*
1--------------2-----------------------------3-------------------- 4--------------5	

Can You Challenge Your View to Find a Better Balance?

I have found that most of us don't even realize where we sit on this scale. We are influenced by the mindset of our family and environment to either expect the worst or look to a more positive view of the future. No one is asking you to be Pollyanna and just assume that everything will be fine. However, I have found that a fighting spirit, which is necessary with cancer, needs hopeful optimism. Can you identify who in your world is an example of a more optimistic view of the world? Who is a realistic optimist? How will you let this person be helpful to you?

Pessimism leads to weakness, optimism to power.

—William James

Positive Self-Talk: Affirmations

Affirmations challenge your negative self-statements that can limit your happiness and well-being. I am not suggesting that a positive statement is a quick fix for self-doubt and poor self-esteem. However, when you are constantly bombarding yourself with what is wrong with you, doubt and insecurity will be the result. Here are some tips to help you write an affirmation that can feel right for you.

Tool: How to Write Your Personal Affirmation

1. Pick an area in your life you want to focus on (e.g., your health, your relationship, your work, or your piece of mind).
2. Decide what you want to occur in this area of your life. What is the end result you are seeking?
3. Formulate a first-person statement that
    affirms what you want (e.g., "I can get stronger"),
    is positive (e.g., "I am relaxed"),
    is worded as if the future is now (e.g., "I am healing"),
    is concise and simple (e.g., "I am hopeful"), and
    is personal and dynamic (e.g., "I value myself and my ability").
4. Experience how the affirmation feels inside you. Don't dismiss the positive, warm feeling with the thought *This is silly*.
5. Repeat your affirmation daily—perhaps even more than once.
6. Turn the final outcome out to your sense of a higher power.

Sometimes we get in our own way and don't always know what is best for us. Releasing your request into the hands of a loving presence is the letting go we all need to practice. Perhaps for you, a higher power has a religious focus. A strong commitment to a faith community is important for many women. Many find solace in giving their future up to their "God." For others who do not relate to an organized faith community, a higher power is their spiritual connection to something larger than themselves. Perhaps for some, this is the power of love. An affirmation can be a statement of love that you need and deserve to receive. I often tell my patients, "You do not have to be perfect to be worthy of love."

Try creating an affirmation that is right for you. Even if it feels awkward at first, try repeating it for twenty-one days. This is the amount of time needed to begin to form a habit. You might want to pair your affirmation with a small goal that is specific and realistic. For example, you might try pairing "I can get stronger" with "I will go for a walk for twenty minutes three times a week."

Identify a small behavioral goal to focus on for the next twenty-one days that fits well with an affirmation that empowers you. Write it down as the first step in creating change.

_____

_____

Warning: No Guilt Trips Allowed

Although this guide is based on the belief that the mind and body work together in health and illness, cancer is more than mind over matter. Health and disease are complex interactions encompassing genes, biology, environment, and behavior as well as psychological factors. Despite all best efforts, there are no guarantees. You might feel as if you are trying to do whatever you can to feel better. You are trying to eat well, exercise, be hopeful, and be connected to others. You might still feel discouraged and frustrated. There is no easy cause-and-effect logic with cancer. If you are having a rough day either physically or emotionally, no guilt trips! A tough day with lots of doubt and negative thinking can be just that. It is one more turn in a curving road you are traveling on this journey. Sometimes we all need to just whine and complain. No one is always positive. Try to give yourself some compassion rather than harsh judgment. Guilt leads only to either anger or depression. Just try to take one step at a time to move forward.

Taking in the Good

Your brain is wired to identify danger and store those reactions for future security. As such, you learn faster from pain than pleasure. This negativity bias helped our ancestors identify the dangers in the environment and survive to pass their genes on to the next generation. Anticipating that things will go wrong is normal and usual for all of us. We remember what went wrong and more frequently forget what went right. Hurt and pain stick, while joy and happiness can easily slip away. We must find ways to train our brains to create the circuits to help those positive experiences stick in our minds and thoughts. The circuits in your brain can be altered. Dr. Richard Hanson, a neuropsychologist, talks about how to take in the good in an intentional way to help rewire your brain.

Tool: How to Take in the Good

- **H: Have** a positive experience. Create a small daily pleasure. It can be as simple as taking a warm bath, watching a sunset, watching your children play, or sitting in front of a fire.
- **E: Enrich** this experience. Feel it in your body, or try moving your body to increase the sense of the positive. Perhaps try sitting or standing up straight to feel stronger. Pull your shoulders down, soften your belly, or let your face relax, and breathe. Savor this positive feeling for ten to thirty seconds. Think about why it is good to feel this positive experience.
- **A: Absorb** the experience to help it sink into your memory. Let the positive become one long moment of appreciation and joy. Just be with the positive feeling, and breathe deeply to let it sink in even more.
- **L: Link** this positive experience to other times that are difficult and negative, so it can soothe the negative. When you have this positive experience, remember that although there are tough times, you are now feeling the richness of this positive experience.

The HEAL tool is one you must use over and over again. Your brain can rewire and change. As Dr. Hanson states, "Neurons that fire together wire together." Use this tool to keep rewiring your brain for well-being. It's not a quick one-time fix but a tool to continue to use each and every day.

What is one way you can practice the HEAL tool today? Can you find one small positive situation right in front of you and begin to let it sink in? Focus outside yourself on someone you care about or perhaps the natural world around you. Soak in the beauty for just a few extra minutes. Shift your attention in the service of your own healing.

Spirit Mileposts on the Lonely Route

Lesson Learned from My Patients

Life is not fair. People do not always get what they deserve. Bad things happen to good people. It is up to me to sort out how I am going to accept what is, rather than focusing on what should be. Staying stuck in blame toward others or myself keeps me from living more fully with an open heart and compassion.

Cancer brings much change and loss. The impact is like a stone dropped into a pond of water: the ripples spread out to all in your world. The way you did things before, the relationships you had, and the roles you played in your life might no longer work the way they did before cancer. You might recognize that you are holding on to old hurts and resentments that are weighing you down. You might carry guilt about how cancer has created demands on your family. Make sure you are not blaming the victim: you. When you spend time focusing and caring for yourself you can gain a clearer sense of what you need to heal. Taking care of yourself is not selfish. Giving yourself time to hear the voice inside you will help you find your compass for moving forward. This is not a quick fix but requires you to be patient with yourself. Letting go is never easy. Letting go of what should have or might have been and accepting what is can be hard when life does not go as you want. What does letting go really mean?

Sogyal Rinpoche, in *The Tibetan Book of Living and Dying*, discusses that we often think that change means loss and suffering. He states that learning to live is learning to let go and work with change.

Tool: Letting Go

- Find a coin to represent the object you are grasping for in your life.
- Hold it tightly in your fist.
- Extend your arm with your palm facing the ground. When you let go, what happens?
- Now turn your palm upward to face the sky, and place the coin in your palm.
- Leave your palm open. The coin is still yours. How does it feel different with your palm up?

Grasping and holding tightly to what was or how it should be can bring pain and frustration. Trying to allow life to proceed and opening up to the universe and all it has to offer might change how you feel. Accepting the impermanence of life and relishing your life without grasping is a challenging goal for us all. Cancer can be a powerful teacher that forces you to change and let go of what was or should have been.

All of us struggle with letting go of what we hoped or planned for that could not or did not actually come to pass. Denise, a thirty-two-year-old single woman, struggled with her inability to have children after chemotherapy. After giving herself time to grieve the loss, she was then able to define *mothering* and how she might care for others. For her, letting go meant moving forward in her education and focusing on working with disabled children and their families. She was able to create a meaningful career for herself and eventually married a man with children who became her family.

I have worked with other women with fertility issues after treatment who decided they would try to adopt to create the family they desired. They had to let go and loosen their grip on what might have been to free themselves to begin a new vision of their lives. This letting go takes time. There might be triggers that bring up feelings of loss that continue to be painful. Time can heal loss, but what you do with that time is what moves your healing forward.

Below are some thoughts (author unknown) about how letting go is vital to healing in our lives. The message is filled with wisdom and challenge. Can you see how these examples play out in your life?

To Let Go

To let go is not to stop caring; it's recognizing I can't do it for someone else.

To let go is not to enable, but to allow learning from natural consequences.

To let go is not to fight powerlessness, but to accept that the outcome is not in my hands.

To let go is not to try and change or blame others; it's to make the most of myself.

To let go is not to care for; it's to care about.

To let go is not to fix; it's to be supportive.

To let go is not to judge; it's to allow another to be a human being.

To let go is not to try and arrange outcomes, but to allow others to affect their own destinies.

To let go is not to be protective; it's to permit another to face their own reality.

To let go is not to regulate anyone, but to strive to become what I dream I can be.

To let go is not to fear less; it's to love more.

Will you complete this request?

Just for today, I will let go of _____.

Think of one small concern that causes you stress and emotional pain that you can let go of just for today. Notice how this affects your overall sense of well-being.

_____

_____

Letting Go of Hurt and Disappointments

You have had times when you were hurt, disappointed, or challenged. Someone treated you unfairly, was deceitful, or even lied to you. Perhaps you think that getting cancer was not fair or just. The reality is that life is not fair! *Bad Things Happen to Good People* by Harold Kushner is more than just a book. It's a fact. Life presents simple unexpected situations, such as "I want the traffic to be one way, and it isn't," to more serious situations, such as "I want to be healthy and able to do what I want, and now I can't."

Basically, the mindset can be summed up with "I did not get something I wanted. I am upset." You feel resentment because things are different from the way you thought they should be. Holding on to this frustration and hurt brings you pain. One way to think about the ability to make peace with *no* is forgiveness for either yourself or others. Forgiveness is the open-heartedness of moving forward—accepting without prejudice and being willing to give the next moment a chance. Forgiveness is a process that is not a quick fix, no matter how minor or serious your disappointment or loss.

The beginning steps to forgiveness are as follows:

1. Acknowledge your hurt or loss, whether it was done to you or happened through no fault of your own.
2. You must feel your feelings, even if there is some sense of suffering. Life deals some hard blows, and loss is part of life, even if painful.
3. Select a few caring people in your life to know about your situation who will provide you the support you need. This support system

might also include a professional if you feel you need that type of support.

How do you create a hurt or grievance?

1. You take offense at another's behavior or your situation.
2. You blame the other person or the situation for how you feel.
3. You create a grievance story and think about it way too often. The story takes up too much rent-free space in your mind. You focus on what is wrong and pay little attention to what might help you feel stronger.

Remember, anger can

- be useful and necessary when you have been mistreated, in danger, or threatened;
- remind you that a problem needs attention;
- keep you stuck and limit clear, constructive thinking; and
- create a stress response within your body.

Are you stuck with an old anger or hurt that keeps you feeling like a victim? Can you describe this situation and think of what you might do to move out of the victim role?

_____

_____

Tool: Ways to Move Forward with Forgiveness

1. Know exactly how you feel about what has happened, and be able to say what about the situation is not OK. Tell a few trusted friends about it.
2. Commit to doing what you need to do to feel better. Forgiveness is something you do for yourself, not others.

3. Forgiveness is not forgetting. This might mean you choose not to stay connected or condone the behavior of the one who hurt you. Your goal is to find your own peace, take the hurt less personally, and change your grievance story.
4. Get perspective. Right now, your distress is coming from hurt thoughts and feelings of suffering. Forgiveness can help heal those hurt feelings.
5. The moment you feel upset, practice some form of simple stress management to calm your body and mind. (Remember your breath.)
6. Identify the rules you have for how others should behave and how they should treat you. You can hope for health, love, peace, and prosperity and work hard to achieve them.
7. Put energy into finding a new way to get your goals met rather than focusing on how you were hurt.
8. A life well lived is the best revenge. Forgiveness brings power to you.
9. Change your grievance story to remind you of the heroic choice to forgive.

There are many ways people have the potential to be hurtful and unkind to each other. A number of women I have worked with have had to manage relationships that were broken long before cancer. They could not look to their partners for support in managing the daily responsibilities of life. By taking the risk to directly address their needs, some decided to leave their relationships. Others put their energy into finding support and validation through organizations, careers, friends, or volunteering. They focused their energy on creating change in their lives.

We do not forget the pain that others can cause. It is, however, up to each of us to find a way to let the hurt take up less rent-free space in our hearts and minds.

Rebecca, a sixty-year-old married woman, began a new chemotherapy for her metastatic cancer. She felt fatigued and fearful and spent most of her time on the couch. Her spouse had a long history of alcohol problems. She was less able to deny and avoid his behavior as her own life became more limited and isolated. She would not respond to friends who tried to text or call her and became more depressed. She finally was convinced to seek counseling. She saw clearly that she could not depend on her husband, but she was unable to leave the marriage because of her need for medical insurance. She agreed to attend Al-Anon meetings, which provided her some understanding of herself and her marriage. She realized she had to refocus her energy and attention on herself and stop trying to change her spouse or his behavior. She could only change herself but needed other supportive relationships to help her cope and reclaim her life.

Over time, her spouse took up less rent-free space in her daily life. She continued to feel sadness at the emptiness of her marriage but focused her energy on those who were able to support her. Forgiveness was a long process. It is a gift you give to yourself.

Forgiveness takes time. You can choose to forgive and not continue to have a relationship with the other person. You are motivated to forgive when you admit to yourself that your hurt and anger are making you feel sick and you no longer want to carry that pain. The hurt might not completely disappear, but it becomes more background noise as you focus on what is nurturing and healthy for you in your relationships with others.

You might find that forgiving yourself is more difficult than forgiving others. We all make mistakes. It is important to admit your mistakes, learn from them, and feel reasonable regret. However, most—particularly women—keep beating themselves up far beyond what is healthy or useful. That inner critic blows up your mistakes and overwhelms your inner protector, who can put events into perspective and encourage you to be more generous in spirit with yourself. Here are some helpful steps to move toward being more compassionate with yourself.

Tool: Steps to Self-Forgiveness

1. Imagine someone in your life who has cared about you and been kind to you.
2. Try to stay with that feeling of being cared about, and identify some simple facts about what your good qualities are. This will help you face whatever needs forgiving.

3. Acknowledge the facts: what you did, what you were thinking at the time, the specific context, and the impact it had on you and others.

4. Be honest with yourself, even if the truth is painful to admit.

5. What happened can be sorted into moral faults, lack of skill, and everything else.

6. Tell yourself, "I am not responsible for _____ and _____." You cannot be responsible for others' inaccurate interpretations or overreactions.

7. Sort out how you will learn from your mistake and make clear amends.

8. Appreciate the efforts you are making. From a place of more compassion, not criticism, try to identify if there is anything more you should do to make amends.

9. Actively forgive yourself by saying, "I forgive myself for____. I take responsibility and have done what I could to make this better."

You might need to go through these self-forgiveness steps over and over again for them to truly sink in so you can move forward. Remember that you can be a more giving and generous person to others if you are less critical and judgmental of yourself. Forgiveness creates more open space and tenderness inside you. We change through love, not criticism. Open yourself up to the peace that can come with self-forgiveness and self-compassion. Working to become kinder and more compassionate toward yourself is a vital part of how you can begin to heal and nourish your spirit.

Is there one specific critical thought you have about yourself or something you have done that you might try using these steps to forgive yourself?

_____

_____

You Need Hope

Hope is a state of mind—a dimension of the spirit and soul—and does not depend only on the present situation. It is not the same as optimism or joy that things are going well. Hope is not dependent on any particular outcome. We cannot survive without hope.

Life is constantly changing, and as it does, your goals have to change. What you hope for must change as the events of your life (and illness) change. If you live with cancer, you must define goals for yourself that have a future focus. Although the future is unknown, your goals can adjust and change as your life does. When times get tough and the future feels uncertain, keep your focus small. You might put your energy into seeking deeper connection in your relationships, managing physical pain more effectively, staying well to attend an important event, or growing in your knowledge or skill in a particular subject. Whatever is important to you now should be the focus of your hope and your goals.

Hope is even more basic to human nature than faith. Some have said faith is based on hope. Your faith beliefs or formal religious practices may be a source of hope for you. Faith and hope both include a sense of trust. Your faith comes from your life experiences, reason, and trusted sources or from just what feels right inside you. Sometimes faith is a bold choice—to believe. Faith fuels hope and optimism and encourages action that can build more faith. Hope has been said to be a prayer without the formality. Hope is in the realm of spirit and a dimension of the spirit anchored beyond the horizon. It is vital to seek ways to nurture your hope and have future goals. Hopelessness leads to helplessness. Hope gives you strength to weather the storms.

- What brings you hope?
- Where do you feel the energy of hope, and from whom do you receive it?
- What situations or relationships drain you of hope? Can you in any way alter your time with those people and seek out those who build your hope?
- Do you find hope in prayer, meditation, inspirational reading, writing, or being in nature?

Tool: Building Your Hope Muscle

1. Identify words you can say to yourself that focus on succeeding. What self-talk encourages you forward?
2. Think of goals and setbacks as challenges, not failures.
3. Remember past successes. You have had these even if you feel cancer is a different kind of challenge than you have faced before in your life.
4. Look for stories of others' successes in books and movies or on the web.
5. Find friends to discuss your goals with.
6. Find role models you can identify with who are inspirations for hope.
7. Maintain your physical strength as much as you can.
8. Reward yourself for small goals.
9. Establish new alternative goals when you can't attain blocked goals.

Rose, a forty-two-year-old, was one of the first breast cancer patients in Virginia in the mid-1980s to have what was then an experimental bone marrow transplant. She was a young mother who was strongly motivated to live for her daughters. Her cancer journey led her to divorce her husband after years of emotional emptiness. She put her energy into raising her daughters and developing her business and community focus. She organized a support group, recognizing that her unique story of thriving and surviving was a source of hope to others. Many of my patients have found a sense of purpose and hope for the future by volunteering their time to their community. Feeling as if you can make even a small difference to another is life affirming. Being able to bring hope to another is a gift we give to ourselves.

Identify where you gain hope and from which people or situations. Can you commit to spend some time to seek out what you need to feel more hope? It is also important to know who in your world brings hurt, disappointment, and negativity. If you can, limit your time with these individuals, and increase your time with those who inspire. Is there some specific way you can commit to building hope as you move forward on your healing journey?

_____

_____

Seeking Health While Facing Cancer

Although life has presented you the challenge of cancer, you have choices as to how you will allow cancer to affect your life. Although you cannot always control external events, you can take charge of how you choose to focus your time and thoughts at each moment. I want you to think about how you can bring health to your life even in the face of cancer. Health is what you do for yourself. It is not just given but must be learned.

Look at this idea from Reverend Stan Hampton of Palo Alto, California:

> What is Health?
>
> **H:** Honesty
> **E:** Energy
> **A:** Acceptance
> **L:** Love
> **T:** Trust
> **H:** Hope

Honesty involves looking at yourself and others truthfully with open eyes. This is not always easy. When times are tough, it is easy to want to run from what is difficult but real. Not only do we need honesty from others, including doctors and those we depend on, but we also need to be willing to face what is happening with compassionate, loving eyes.

Energy can be in short supply when you are not feeling well either physically or emotionally. Seeking out others and situations that bring you more positive energy is important. Along with the physical movement that helps generate vitality, energy is a metaphor for moving forward. Be aware of the situations and people around you who drain your energy, and reduce the time and space you give to them.

Acceptance is the next component. When you or those you love have to face the fearful, challenging aspects of illness, you want life to be different. You question how to make it better. Although developing tools to manage and cope helps you feel a greater sense of personal control, there is a need to just accept what is happening and not try to run away or deny the reality of the situation. Acceptance is not the same as giving up. By freeing up the energy that holding on and denying robs from your daily life, you can focus on how to increase your options for healing.

Love is a word that means something different to each of us. Self-love is not selfish. Extending compassion and self-love to yourself allows you to create change and growth. Giving to others and showing love are a lot easier when you have a full heart.

Trust is the next component. Having a trusting relationship with those you need, such as your doctors and family, is vital to good health. Trust can be broken easily, but rebuilding takes time. Pay attention to how you need to behave in order to trust yourself. With trust, you can feel stronger and more able to face the challenges life throws at you.

Hope must change as your life circumstances change. However, finding something, no matter how small, to hope for is vital to managing any challenging life event. Seek inspiration wherever you can, including nature, art, religion, or other people, but never stop seeking that ray of hope.

As you are leaving the Rough and Lonely Route on your journey, try identifying with each letter in the above HEALTH, and define how you can increase this quality in your daily life. Choose one behavior to commit to for each letter, and write it down now.

```
╔══════════════════════════════════════════════╗
║            Committed Action Contract           ║
╚══════════════════════════════════════════════╝
```

I will be more honest with myself and others by

_____.

I will increase my energy this week by

_____.

I will show myself more acceptance by

_____.

I will identify and embrace sources of love in my life by

_____.

I will trust myself and listen to my inner voice by

_____.

I will bring more hope to my daily life by

_____.

I will start these changes by

_____(specific date).

You can bring more health to your daily life with each small step you are willing to take. Please just begin with one step forward.

This chapter has given you tools to care for your body to reduce the impact of treatment and the disease process. Identifying the thoughts that keep you stuck enables you to see what is possible and take control of what you can change in your daily life. Letting go of hurt and anger allows you to move forward with a greater sense of hope for the future.

3

You Are Not Traveling Alone

Navigate Together

- Develop an understanding of your sensuality and sexuality.
- Gain skills in effectively communicating your needs.
- Build your compassion and sense of gratitude.

Although you are the one coping with cancer, those who know, love, and care about you are also affected. Cancer is like throwing a rock into a stream, with the ripples creating waves for all those who love you. However, feeling guilty and responsible for the challenges your illness might create for others is not the way to cope or manage this journey. It is, however, important for you to have more awareness and understanding of how your family and friends can travel this road with you.

Family can mean your partner, biological relatives, friends, or whoever in your life you want to include on your cancer journey. This chapter begins with a focus on your body, recognizing how cancer might have altered your most intimate relationship. Whether you are married to a man or woman, single and dating, or living alone, your understanding and feelings about your body are an integral part of your healing journey. You may or may not choose to be sexually active; however, knowing how your body functions can empower you to make the best choices for you. This chapter also provides tools to improve your ability to listen and communicate more effectively with partners, family, and friends to build more supportive relationships. By identifying your needs and finding gratitude in your life, you will create a stronger connection to yourself and others.

So let's begin and open the door to what might be a difficult topic to explore.

Your Body and Physical Intimacy

> **Lessons Learned from My Patients**
>
> How I define myself as a woman must change as my body and life changes. I cannot get stuck in trying to live up to society's views but must be clear about my own standards to maintain my self-respect and self-worth. How my sexuality is lived is based on my emotional needs for connection and intimacy as well as my body image and physical needs.

Cancer changes not only your physical body but also your image of yourself as a woman. Your body image is how you see yourself and what you believe about your appearance. Changes after treatment, such as changes in your breast, hair loss, weight loss or gain, or swelling in other parts of your body, might influence how attractive you feel. Women struggle with not wanting to feel exposed and "look like a cancer patient." One of the most powerful moments for one patient was being able to walk out of my office without her wig. She felt strong enough in her own skin to just be who she was in that moment and feel no embarrassment. She could now choose how she wanted to manage her baldness.

I have learned that each woman has her own unique emotional attachment to her breasts. For some, loss of a breast can cause them to feel less feminine and attractive. For others, this loss is just a necessary part of removing the cancer from their bodies. Many want reconstruction, while others never choose to do so. Each woman must have the opportunity to decide what is best for her and not allow others to make that choice.

Surgery, treatment, and their impact on your body image and sexuality play a major role in how your intimate relationships move forward after a diagnosis. Sexuality is a complex issue for us all. During active treatment, being sexually intimate was probably the last thing you thought or cared about. It is, however, for some, an issue of concern, especially after the initial phases of treatment are completed. Changes in your body image, menopausal symptoms, overall fatigue, and worry can sap any desire for physical or sexual contact. The change in sexual relationships after treatment is one of the most challenging issues for many of the women I have seen in therapy. How important is a sexually intimate relationship in your life? You must be honest with yourself about what you want and need in your sexual life.

If you are not interested in exploring your sexuality, feel free to skip over this section of the chapter. You must feel free to choose if you do or do not want to be sexually active. Sexuality is just one form of sensuality. Throughout the guide are many tools to connect to your sensuality, which is the enjoyment and pursuit of physical pleasures. It's important to find ways to connect to any and all of your physical senses. Sight, smell, hearing, taste, and touch are all options for increased well-being.

I know that sexuality is a difficult topic for many women to talk about with their medical teams. This section is meant not to replace your need for medical consultation to assist in your physical and sexual needs but to help you relearn how your body works, reconnect with your body, and redefine your sexuality and expectations. You must be direct enough with your questions so that your medical team can provide you options to meet your specific needs.

You might decide that you and your partner need further help in moving forward as a couple and seek professional help. Although I hope to provide you with some helpful resources, relationships are hard work and often require an objective third party to find a new balance for a couple after the challenges of cancer. I have seen how the challenges of cancer can increase the strength of a relationship or tear it down. After many years as a couples' therapist, I can clearly state that each relationship is unique and complicated and cannot be easily understood by others. The strength of any partnership is challenged by the many changes that cancer demands of each person. Overall, if you and your partner can work together as a team, the strength of the relationship can endure the challenge.

Clearly, your own needs as well as the needs of your partner will affect your motivation to explore the sexual aspects of your life. I believe your sexuality is a natural part of your life force. It is a reflection of how you feel in your body, your beliefs about your body, and how you relate to this part of yourself. Cancer has affected your physical body, but how you attempt to feel more connected to and accepting of your body and yourself as a sexual person is up to you. It is important to educate yourself.

Love is a matter of chemistry, but sex is a matter of physics.

—Author unknown

A Lesson about Sexual Functioning

Following are some definitions of sexual functioning:

- *Desire* is the anticipation and feeling that you deserve sexual pleasure.
- *Arousal* is being receptive to and responding in your body to touching and genital stimulation (e.g., how much you lubricate and how your nipples enlarge).
- *Orgasm* is letting go and allowing the arousal to naturally culminate in climax.
- *Satisfaction* is feeling emotionally and physically bonded after your sexual experience.

Desire

Sexual desire in women is more complex than male sexual desire. There are some basic components that might help you as you try to understand your desire (or lack thereof) for sexual intimacy.

- *Drive* is the biology of it all. You have experienced many changes in how your body functions. Changes in hormones, brain chemistry (neurotransmitters involved in regulation of your mood), medication, and changes to your physical body are just some of the ways your desire might be affected.
- *Expectations* and *beliefs* you have about sexuality and your body are based on your past experiences, your culture, your religion, and society. Although the world may have changed regarding women's sexuality, how you think and feel about your own sexuality might change much more slowly than the worldview around you. What are the best choices that respect your beliefs and values? Knowing what is best for you requires some focused thinking. Knowing how others have influenced you is an important first step in understanding what is best for you. Can you identify who might have been a healthy role model of a woman comfortable with her sexuality in your life? How much are you comparing yourself to external media standards for evaluating your attractiveness or sexual appeal?
- *Motivation* is about how much you want to change your physical intimate relationship with your partner. You and your partner might be in agreement on a limited physical sexual relationship. Clearly, a difference in desire between any couple is often an issue that brings them into counseling. You need to be honest with yourself about how much you want to change your sexual behavior.

In thinking about why you want to have sex, are you motivated to please your partner, or do you just want to avoid feeling guilty for saying no? Do you feel motivated to create more closeness with your partner and make them feel good? Do you just want to avoid conflict and try to keep your partner from being angry or disappointed?

When you have a positive motivation, your relationship as well as your desire is stronger. This is the same for both men and women. It matters to most partners why you want to have sex. It is important to take the time to lead with what you want instead of what you don't want to happen.

Tool: Identify Your Sexual Turnoffs

What can cause you to turn off to sexual intimacy with your partner?

- Physical pain or discomfort associated with intercourse must be addressed with your physician.
- If you feel pressured or threatened in any way or hurt or disappointed with your partner, your desire will disappear.
- If you feel guilty about any changes or challenges your cancer has created, you will probably want to isolate from your partner physically (and emotionally).
- Anxiety over your performance or anticipating how you will perform will reduce desire.
- Fear of pregnancy will limit desire.
- If your image of your body is poor or you feel embarrassed at being seen, you will fear rejection and not desire physical contact.
- Nonstop thinking about anything other than what you are doing with your partner interferes with your ability to be spontaneous during sex.
- Feelings and thoughts of shame based on past experiences—abuse, sexually transmitted disease, or having been ridiculed—will destroy desire. Shaming is blaming the victim: you.

Can you identify any of the above turnoffs as playing a role in your lack of desire?

_____

_____

Resolving any of these concerns will take time. You must be honest with yourself about how motivated you are to look at your sexual relationship and what you are willing to do to make any change. Plan small steps to help yourself feel comfortable with the expectation that you will make gains and then possibly relapse to old behavior. You need a trusted listener, such as a close friend, a therapist, or, ideally, your partner. If change is to happen, you need the support of your partner to move toward a safe and comfortable sexual relationship.

Sexual intimacy requires being open and comfortable, sharing pleasure, and reducing tension to lessen the stressors of life. Men as well as women can perform sexually without feeling intimate. In a committed relationship, sex can be based on need, feelings, the situation, and time constraints. Sex between partners can be warm and tender, erotic, lustful, and short or long in duration. Emotional intimacy and sexual intimacy are not the same, but both are part of a healthy relationship. Emotional intimacy requires respect and trust and is not the same as romantic love.

The prescription to create a vital sexual desire and satisfying sexuality is as follows:

- *Emotional intimacy.* What are some necessary conditions that help you feel physically free, safe, and secure with your partner?
- *Nondemanding pleasure.* Do you spend time touching without the expectation that every touch must lead to intercourse? Touch for touch's sake.
- *Erotic scenes and techniques.* Can you develop ways to excite each other that maintain the safety and security you need?

Love is a canvas furnished by Nature and embroidered by Imagination.

—Voltaire

Touch: The Bridge for Sexual Desire

Touch that has no sense of threat or demand and shows respect for each partner's personal boundaries is necessary for sexual desire. Nondemanding pleasuring is cooperative and respectful and accepting of what each person wants. Like the gears of a vehicle, touching has many different gears. These are as follows:

- Affectionate touch is friendly, such as hugging and gentle touch, with clothes on.
- Sensual touch includes cuddling, embracing, holding, and soothing and can involve nongenital touching.

- Playful touch is comfortable and secure, mixing genital and nongenital touching.
- Erotic touch can be manual, oral, rubbing, and erotic stimulation to orgasm.
- Intercourse touch is a genital connection and bond.

To create an intimate, safe team for all sexual gears, the following must apply:

- Both partners can stop or veto anything that is uncomfortable.
- Touch needs to be comfortable and safe.
- Clear, specific communication about your needs is vital. You have to be able to ask for what you want and clarify what you don't want. No mind reading!

Many times, when a couple stops having sexual contact, they stop touching each other in other caring, affectionate ways. Touch does not have to be a prelude to intercourse. Loving touch is important for us all. I have found that you might have to help your partners understand nondemanding pleasuring by telling them what you do or do not need from them. Not every physical encounter has to result in orgasm. Many men have been socialized not to express feelings of tenderness and vulnerability. Society tells men that a sign of their manhood is to be sexually active. Therefore, many different emotional needs for men are met through sex. Finding ways as a couple to share emotional connection outside of sexual activity requires you both to work at creating shared pleasurable time together outside the bedroom.

How to Create Bridges to Desire

We all need to look forward to whatever we are planning to do. This goes for sexual plans as well. What brings you pleasure? What behavior or environments help you feel more open and turn you on to being sexual with either yourself or your partner? Your first answer might be that you are not sure, but think about what helps you feel more playful, builds fantasy, feels erotic, or releases tension.

In real life, we have to plan intimate dates. How can you create more erotic scenes with your partner? Consider sexy movies, fantasy, mirrors, positions, lotion, and certain muscle movements. What could turn you on? Can you bring some variety to your time together? How open are you to exploring any of the many ways to be more sexually adventuresome? How will you commit the time to be together? The important point in being open to erotic scenes and techniques is that it must be voluntary, pleasure-oriented, and mutual, with no pressure. Are you willing to explore what beliefs or attitudes keep you from feeling more open and comfortable to express yourself with more freedom? What messages do you tell yourself that hold you back from being more spontaneous and opening yourself up to physical pleasure and touch?

Remember, not every sexual event with your partner has to rate a ten. There is no set amount of time you should be intimate, and you should not define your time together as a failure if one or the other does not achieve orgasm. Orgasm does not have to be the goal.

Owning your sexuality is accepting that your partner cannot excite you unless you are willing, know what you need, and communicate it. You must be an active participant.

Accept that you deserve sexual pleasure. Sexuality is giving and receiving pleasure-oriented touching. Thinking about pleasure, not performance, helps build desire.

How you view your body and how you evaluate your attractiveness are central to feeling desirable to your partner. I know you might look different and don't always feel you are at your best during and after cancer treatment. The physical changes and losses are hard to accept. Finding ways to increase your self-esteem with various self-care tools is important in increasing how desirable you feel as a woman. When partners are exposed early to your physical scars, relationships can move forward. Most partners are more concerned about your health or not hurting you with their touch than how your chest or body looks. However, how you feel about your body is vital to feeling comfortable and safe with physical intimacy. Whatever changes you have had in your body shape or size and how you want to physically connect with your partner are important issues for the safety and health of your important relationship.

Many of the women I have seen struggle with being able to be mentally present when they are with their partners or when they choose to explore their bodies alone. It is difficult to tune into what your body is feeling when you are not focusing on the sensations that arise and are thinking about what needs to be done tomorrow. There is no sense of desire when being with your partner is just one more job to check off your schedule. Realistically, however, some scheduling for intimate time together usually needs to happen when lives are busy.

Can you identify a positive role model of a woman in your life who was comfortable with her sexuality? How did she express her sexuality? Are there societal standards you might challenge as to how you need to look appealing and sexual?

_____

_____

What Is Arousal?

Arousal is your physical body's response to stimulation. It involves maintaining rhythmic clitoral stimulation with erotic stimulation of your breasts, mons, or anal area. Being able to let go and feel aroused involves psychological, sexual, and relationship factors. What turns off your desire to be physically intimate also reduces your physical arousal.

Although treatment effects and changes in hormones can reduce your ability to become physically aroused, challenges in your emotional relationship with your partner also affect your arousal. Although sexual contact might be different after cancer, you can still find ways to explore being sexually connected with your partner. What might turn you off emotionally and reduce your arousal?

Tool: Poisons for Your Arousal

- Relationship struggles with your partner
- Physical changes and side effects from treatment (e.g., medication, menopause, and pain)
- Lack of desire

- Poor body image
- Lack of time and privacy
- Stress in your work or home life

Although female arousal is usually physically slower than males', you need to know your body and what feels good to you and communicate it to your partner. Your physician might suggest options for lubrication, given the effects of treatment, but you also have to know your body well enough to identify what does or does not feel good for you.

How can you develop your sexual voice? How can you state what you need? What kind of stimulation is best for you? What erotic techniques (e.g., vibrators, fingers, or oral sex) are you able to ask for? Many women have a difficult time asking for what they need. Finding a way to accept what is right for you involves listening to your own internal voice and not that of others.

Many women have never masturbated, often for reasons related to social, religious, or cultural beliefs. We are all products of our past experiences regarding our sexual feelings. Clearly, if you have been sexually abused in any way, you might struggle with finding your voice. Letting go of shame or guilt frees you to accept that sexuality is a normal life force. There are many advantages to knowing your own body, which can be learned through your own exposure to your body. The excellent book *For Yourself* by Dr. Lonnie Barbach is a good resource. Accepting your sexuality as a normal expression of your life force can reduce shame and help you become an active member of your intimate team.

Can you identify what turns your arousal off? What is one small change you might make to increase your ability to tune into your body in a more pleasurable way?

Orgasm, the Big *O*

Orgasm is the progressive increased experience of sexual excitement and tension followed by the irresistible, compelling release and subsequent calm and tranquility. Women can be nonorgasmic, singly orgasmic, or multiorgasmic, and orgasm can occur during pleasuring, intercourse, or afterplay. Sex is not and should not be a performance to have any specific type or number of orgasms. I have found with couples that this fact often is easier for women to accept than for their male partners. However, there must be enough physical arousal for orgasm to happen. There is no scientific data to validate a difference between clitoral and vaginal orgasms. The feeling of satisfaction from the letting go of orgasm depends on your own preferences, experiences, and values. Having an orgasm each time you are with your partner or choose to pleasure yourself is an unrealistic expectation. You are not a sexual machine, and your sexuality is more variable and complex than male orgasm.

Desire and emotional satisfaction are more important than orgasm. The important goal is to share intimacy, pleasure, and eroticism. Quality over quantity leads to satisfaction.

Sexuality is a complex topic. Don't hesitate to get professional help when and if you and your partner are struggling. In couples' counseling, the patient is the relationship. Look for a therapist who has experience in working with couples, as it is a different process than individual counseling. Sexual issues in your relationship have different causes; however, it often takes both individuals to work on the issues to create a more satisfying, meaningful sexual experience for both partners.

Tool: The CREST Tool for an Improved Sexual Life

- **C: Creativity.** How might you bring more joy, playfulness, and variety to your physical relationship? What might help you get outside your head and into your body to experience the pleasure of touch? What is the best environment for you to relax and direct your thoughts to be in the present moment?
- **R: Respect.** How can you show respect to your partner, and what do you need to feel valued and respected? You probably want to

be spoken to, touched, and appreciated outside the bedroom to feel the respect you need to free yourself sexually. Do you respect yourself enough to ask for what you need and to take the time for self-care to feel better about yourself?

- **E: Excitement.** We all need variety and things to look forward to, especially when we are challenged with illness. Trying something different takes some motivation but may be an important first step in changing old, boring patterns and habits.
- **S: Sensitivity.** Feeling you are being treated with kindness and valued for not only what you do but also who you are helps build an intimate team. Paying attention to your partner increases the safety and comfort of being able to enjoy physical intimacy.
- **T: Togetherness.** Finding time to be together as a couple is needed, even though the demands on you both might be great. Your relationship must be a priority. I often say that a relationship is like a garden: it needs tending, or the weeds will overtake it.

Ask yourself the following questions:

- Do you want to take a step to increase your sexual desire? If so, how can self-care and attention to feeling more positive about your body image help build your desire?
- Are you ready to open up the conversation with your partner about your sexual relationship?
- What do you need to do to effectively manage the physical changes from treatment and get the medical help you might need to improve your sexual relationship?

Identifying what is really happening physically as well as emotionally with your partner is the first place to create change. It is a difficult topic to discuss but can move forward only with open, honest conversation. You can make changes in your own behavior, but a team approach is the most effective way to bring more connection and joy.

In working with my patients, I have found that change can also occur in a relationship if only one person is willing to change behavior. So if your partner is unwilling to try counseling, you can create change for yourself by going alone to talk to someone. I often say that relationships are like a seesaw. If you move one side, the other side will have to move for balance and movement to occur. Be the change you want to see!

What is one small change you want to make to increase your sexual satisfaction?

_____

_____

Mileposts for Open Communication

Lessons Learned from My Patients

Important relationships continue to change as my life and needs evolve. Others cannot know what I need unless I tell them as clearly as I can. How I say what I feel is as important as what I say. Communicating is more about listening than talking. Often, less is more.

Cancer demands that you develop an open mind. The way you think about what is happening to you is central not only to how you feel but also to the quality of your relationships with those around you. Your ability to communicate your thoughts, feelings, and needs will directly influence how you and others manage the changes and demands of cancer. Let's look at some of the important people on your journey and how to communicate more effectively with them.

How to Reach a Win-Win with Others

Relationships are hard work even in the best of times. The stress of cancer creates different needs, opinions, and solutions for each partner. Whatever the topic, here are some important points to remember to get to a win-win result.

The first step in good communication is to set the stage. Create a time and place to talk about important issues when you won't be distracted. Come to this with an attitude of collaboration. Win-win is the goal, but sometimes you might only be able to agree to disagree. If others are not ready to have a conversation, ask them when they might be willing to begin. Give others a chance to have some specific time to think and tell you when they are ready to discuss the issue. Just don't leave it without any set time to follow up (e.g., "I'm not ready to talk now, but I will be in _____ [an hour, tomorrow]"). Most of us have a hard time when we feel our concerns will not even be heard or addressed.

Next, define the problem. Describe what behavior is creating a problem with you. Specify the situation where the problem occurs and how it affects you. For example, "When you withdraw from me when I ask for more help in the house or with the kids, I feel hurt and upset."

Tool: Ten Steps for a Problem-Solving Win-Win Approach

1. Start with a positive statement. This can be thought of as a soft start ("I want to talk to you because our relationship matters to me").
2. Be specific, and describe the behavior. Don't use critical words to describe the other person (e.g., "You are lazy and cold"). Ask yourself: Do you want to express anger, get even, or solve the problem?
3. Avoid being too general by using the words "You always [or never] do that."
4. Express your feelings directly. For example, say, "I feel ...," not "You make me feel ..." Take responsibility for the way you feel. Don't start by blaming the other person. Be brief when you describe the problematic behavior, and don't focus on why you

think the behavior is happening. Discuss one problem at a time. Don't throw the kitchen sink at your partner!

5. Own your part in creating and maintaining the problem by accepting as much responsibility as you truthfully can. Work to be neutral. Any issue between two people can become a power struggle.

6. Summarize what you have heard your partner say before you respond. Try to begin with "Is what I heard you say …" Don't interrupt. Slow down the conversation.

7. Don't make assumptions about your partner. Speak only about what you can observe. Don't mind read or assume you know what they are thinking or feeling. (This is one of the most common issues I see in working with couples. You don't know what someone is thinking unless they tell you. Then you have to believe they are telling you the truth.)

8. Focus on solutions. You both must want change. Ask, "What's going to work for us both?" Compromise, and try to make changes at the same time if possible. Ask yourself, "What do I really want, and what am I willing to settle for?"

9. Discuss the pros and cons of the proposed solution and the costs to both of you.

10. Be specific as to when, how often, and how each of you will remind the other of the changes you have agreed to try to make.

Consider writing down the agreement on a trial run for a specific time, and evaluate how it is going.

I have heard from many couples, "We just don't communicate well." Remember, communication is more about listening than talking.

Communication often stops when you most need contact and support from your significant other. Committing time each and every day to spend some time talking is a vital tool for maintaining connection and intimacy. Following is a tool I recommend for all my patients, originally from the well-known family therapist Virginia Satir.

Tool: The Daily Temperature Reading

Each day, try to set some time aside to do the following:

- Express your appreciation. Find a sincere way to say what you value in your partner. Be aware if you have trouble receiving a compliment. Sometimes all that is needed is "Thank you."

- Share new information. Do you keep to yourself what is going on with you? This can create a lot of assumptions that may or may not be accurate. Connection builds when you share what is important and what is trivial in work, family, or mutual concerns. Remember, no one knows what you are thinking or feeling unless you tell them. No mind reading allowed.

- Take time to ask. If you are unsure what is going on with your partner, take the risk and ask. If you have concerns, let your partner know you just want to share and don't expect them to have the answers or solve your problem. Listening and sharing might be as much as you need. Often, partners feel they must fix the situation, when the women just want to be heard and have others listen. Those closest to you are often into fixing what they think is your problem. As you know, it is not always possible to just fix some of the challenges of cancer. I heard one woman say, "I am the general contractor in my cancer fight, with my spouse as the subcontractor." You are in charge, but have a working team.

- Complain with a request for change. When you need something to change, try to stick to specific behaviors. No blaming or judgment needed. If an issue is too difficult, you might need more time to discuss. Remember, the daily temperature check is not meant for serious conflict resolution.

- Share your hopes and dreams. Don't lose sight of the bigger picture. Your partner can know what you need only if you tell them.

Use these steps to begin daily communication with your significant other. Practice makes all new behavior easier. You can change the temperature of your relationship. Try to think of a specific issue you want to discuss, and take the risk of bringing it up using some of these tools.

_____

_____

How to Resolve and Lessen Conflict with Others

There are some surefire ways to increase conflict when you are trying to have a tough conversation. We all can fall into these pitfalls, which will only lead to feeling awful.

Tool: Conflict Accelerators

1. Blaming others for your feelings might help you justify your anger, but it will accomplish little.
2. Using the words "You should" or "I would" will guarantee the other person does not listen or shuts down to further conversation.
3. If you say, "If only you [or I] had …" when things don't work out, this attitude will bring you guilt or more self-doubt.
4. Your taking responsibility for everyone and everything can allow others to feel no responsibility and isn't accurate. Not everything is about you or because of you and your behavior.
5. Thinking in terms of forever, always, or never or using the words *everyone* or *everything* creates conflict. These words are examples of global all-or-nothing thinking, which leads to helpless or hopeless feelings. Others will tune you out when you begin a conversation this way.

Think about your last disagreement, and honestly try to evaluate which of these pitfalls you have fallen into. Can you commit to changing one small way you act during conflict?

_____

_____

When an Apology Is Needed

As much as you need to be able to ask for what you want, it is also important to be able to recognize when you have hurt another person. None of us is perfect, and cancer creates many stressful situations when you are not at the top of your game. You might feel poorly or irritable and say or do things that hurt others. However, because women often feel responsible for others, they say, "I'm sorry," even when the situation is trivial and not necessary to apologize. When you have truly hurt another person, it is easy to become defensive and feel vulnerable, exposed, and insecure. I will focus on when you have created the offense, but this also applies to those who need to seek your forgiveness.

Tool: How to Give a Real Apology

- Don't make up excuses for why you did or said what you did. No ifs, ands, or buts. An apology requires that you have listened carefully to the hurt party's anger and pain.
- The offended person has the right to decide about forgiving you. You must tolerate the time it takes for someone to do this. Forgiveness is not the same as forgetting, and the injured person must have the time and space to heal.
- To apologize is to express what you said or did directly and clearly. It's not "I'm sorry you feel that way," puts the focus on the person

who has been hurt rather than on you, the offender. You must own the hurt you have caused. The hurt parties need to know you get it. They need to know that their hurt feelings make sense to you.

- As hard as it is to hear, you must listen openly. It takes courage and maturity to put another person or relationship ahead of your need to be right.

- Nondefensive listening is the core of a sincere apology. It takes courage to apologize, but an apology can facilitate health for you and others. We forgive for ourselves because it is part of our own healing.

- This process does not always go well and might not result in repair of the relationship. Knowing you have honestly and openly apologized allows you to try to move forward.

You might be able to identify with Peggy, a fifty-three-year-old mother of two teenage sons, who had completed chemotherapy and radiation and had begun to take tamoxifen. She was not sleeping well and was fatigued and often irritable and angry toward her sons and her husband, Joe. They withdrew from her and spent more time away from home. Peggy came to therapy feeling hurt and alone without the support of her family. As we explored her behavior, she was able to acknowledge her part in this cutoff and asked Joe to schedule some time to talk. She began with a sincere curiosity about what Joe was feeling and showed empathy for how much life had changed for him. She tried to understand how her behavior had pushed him away. She explained why she was sorry and what she planned to do differently. She recognized she needed to find ways to take better care of herself and ask for what she needed with less anger.

By feeling heard, Joe was able to share the challenges he faced as well as the fear he had tried to hide when she was first diagnosed. Although the conversation moved their relationship forward, both recognized that this apology was just a beginning, and follow-through would be ongoing. This was an important first step in bridging the divide between them.

Is there a person in your life whom you need to ask for forgiveness and apologize to? Can you identify what might be standing in your way of reaching out and trying to repair the relationship? Can you see how trying to apologize may be beneficial for you and your health?

_____

_____

Effectively Talk to Others about Your Cancer

Overall, other people want to be helpful and supportive when you have cancer. Most of the time, they just don't know what to say. I am sure each of you can remember certain conversations when others have made unhelpful remarks to you. When people get anxious, they often say what is not appropriate. To assist them in being more helpful to you, consider some of the following tips. (You might even give them this list if you think it will help.)

Tool: Help Others Be a Help to You

The words below might provide helpful responses for you in addressing others' comments about your cancer.

1. Please start by listening, and let me take the lead. Keep your questions short, and be prepared for whatever answer I might give. I don't always want to talk about my cancer.
2. Please don't say, "Everything will be fine," or "We are only given what we can handle." Although I know you want to show me support, these statements feel like a denial of my struggle.
3. Please remember it is not helpful to me to hear about how others you have known have managed or not with their cancer. I am an individual, and comparisons don't usually help.
4. I know you care about me, but please monitor your feelings so as not to overwhelm me. I can't feel guilty about your pain about my cancer.

5. If I don't share every detail of my illness, please don't take it personally. This is not about where you are on my friendship list.
6. It is often helpful to first email or send a note, particularly when I am managing treatment. Please understand if I do not always respond quickly.
7. I know you might not always know what to say and might feel uncertain around me. I don't expect you to take away my emotional pain or fix this.
8. Please remember that the greatest gift you can give me is to just be present and listen.

As you look at this list, try to identify someone in your world whom you need to speak with to improve the relationship. Could any of the examples on this list open up communication that is blocked for you?

_____

_____

The Challenges in Talking with Children

Many women struggle with how and what to say to children when they are diagnosed. Whether you are a mother, grandmother, aunt, or important friend to a young person how you speak to them will matter. Women feel responsible for the safety and well-being of children and struggle with the guilt of how their cancer might be frightening and change their sense of security. With all the important people in your world, honesty is vital. Secrets in any important relationship lead to more secrets and limit trust. Kids read the environment anyway and don't need to feel isolated from their caregivers or those they love. If you are physically and emotionally able to talk to the children in your life, try to be the one to do so. Remember, in talking to children about your cancer, it's OK for you to cry. If you are not sure you can talk to them directly, let someone you trust (e.g., a spouse, relative, or health care provider) be the one to talk to them. Telling them as soon as you can prevents them from having to guess what is creating the changes they are experiencing around them. For children, fantasy can be more frightening than reality.

Remember, children's needs for information differ according to their age.

Children three to five years old are more concerned with the separation from you. They engage in magical thinking and believe that what they wish will come true. Some fear any bad thought or behavior they have had might have caused your cancer. Reassure them they have done nothing to cause your cancer. Use simple, age-appropriate terms in describing your illness. Use the word *cancer*. You might try to find one of the many books published for young children to read to them. Children this age do not yet clearly understand the concept of death.

Children six to eleven years old can become overly concerned with your health. Keep details honest but minimal. Give them enough information to help them deal with their world, trying to be as hopeful as possible. Be sure to prepare young children for a hospital visit and what they might see regarding medical equipment and how you might look tired or sick. Make sure their school knows about your cancer as soon as possible. Let the children know they will be informed of changes to their schedules and will be taken care of when you are feeling ill. You might see them become more childlike in their behavior both at home and at school. Look for changes in eating and sleeping patterns.

Teenagers, who are going through their own process of becoming their own people and more independent, can respond in a variety of ways. Listen to their reactions, and if they do not want to talk or ask questions, don't push it. Some will rebel at the increased need you have for them to help and will act more immaturely. Others will try to be the best helpers possible and become very responsible. Be aware that some young women might worry about their own potential for breast cancer. Others might take the news in stride and show little to no reaction to the changes going on around them in the home. It can be a difficult ride with teens even in the best of situations, as their own emotional balance can be shaky in this developmental stage.

Remember the following:

- Focus on what action is being taken that can give everyone hope.
- Share your feelings, and know it's OK to say, "I don't know."

- Kids observe but often inaccurately interpret what is happening.
- Speak the truth, even if your prognosis is poor. If the child asks if you are dying, consider answering with "I'm not dying right now. Some people die, and others get better. I am doing everything possible to get better." If your condition is terminal, this discussion will have to include other important issues.
- If children show signs of not coping—changes in mood, personality, or sleep; decreased appetite; withdrawal; acting out; or physical complaints for more than two weeks—consider consulting with their doctor to get professional help to help them cope.

Consider a family meeting including the children (if age appropriate) to talk about how everyone is reacting to your illness. The online resource www.caregiver.org can help you plan how to have a meeting.

Setting Clear Boundaries for Communication

Just as your house might have a fence around it to define physical property, you need to protect and define your psychological house. It is natural and healthy to want to ensure your safety and protect what belongs to you. Your personal boundaries are the way you can define yourself, your identity, and your needs. They let others know how far they can go before they must ask permission to go further. They define both your emotional needs and your physical needs.

As a cancer patient, your physical house, or body, is vulnerable to painful procedures that can push against your personal physical boundaries. You might not always have the space you need. You can, however, work to strengthen your emotional house and boundary by identifying and being clear about where your fences need to be set. Fences are not walls. Fences provide limits for others to know your level of comfort and acceptance. Ideally, your fence has a gate for others to come and go. You are not shut off from others. You, however, must be clear on your boundaries when others move into your physical space.

It is hard as a patient to ask for what you need when you feel so dependent and vulnerable. It might only be a minor adjustment in your medical care that you can ask for, but it is important to try to communicate what might be helpful to you. (Something as small as asking to have your blood drawn in another arm is a way to define your boundaries.)

As much as we need to break down barriers and connect with others, it is still important to have our personal fences. Often, those closest to you are the ones who don't respect or react well to your boundaries or fences. When you don't protect yourself or your personal space, you might feel trapped or become angry. For example, others might have unrealistic expectations or demand too much of your time or energy. It is your job to communicate clearly what and where your fences need to be. If you are not sure and send out mixed messages, the boundaries will be confusing to others.

Women especially have a tough time setting boundaries, because they fear they are being selfish. Women also fear that others will become angry and reject them if they say no. It is up to you to keep your time, space, and house safe and free from intruders. It is your job to communicate your fences. When you do, you value yourself and build more satisfying, peaceful relationships with those important to you. Remember, no one knows what you need unless you tell them as clearly and honestly as you can.

Charlene, forty-five years old, had completed her chemotherapy and radiation. Her energy had just begun to return. She wanted to begin to have a more satisfying physical relationship with her husband, Dan. As we talked further about her needs, she was able to identify ways her past sexual life had been less than satisfying for her. She had not been able to tell Dan what she needed to more fully enjoy their intimate time together. She knew she had to be more direct and clear as to how she needed to be touched by him. Sensation in her breasts had changed since her surgery, along with a decrease in her desire. She wanted to spend more time touching without the expectation of intercourse. She was concerned Dan would be hurt by her lack of desire and her honesty about this with him.

Initially, Dan felt a sense of betrayal and hurt. After real conversation, he could appreciate that knowing what Charlene really wanted would increase the pleasure for them both. They could begin an open conversation about how to move forward together sexually as well as emotionally. Working as an intimate team was an important change for them.

Relationships are constantly challenging and require attention and work. When negative emotions surface, such as anger, impatience, or a lack of respect, try using these tools to become more aware and mindful of yourself and the situation.

> Do not learn how to react. Learn how to respond.
>
> —Buddha

Tool: Ways to Respond and Not Just React

- *Stop.* Become aware as soon as you can of the early warning signs of your emotional reaction. Remind yourself to pay attention to this now.
- *Breathe.* Become sensitive to how a relaxed breath can soften your body and allow the negative emotion to soften.
- *Reflect.* Ask yourself, "What old pattern is going on now? What is my reaction calling me to work on? Can I see this situation differently? Is the other person intending to hurt me? Even if they are wrong, can I be more patient or understanding? What is my best insight about this, and what do I want to remember?"
- *Choose.* Ask yourself, "Now that I am more aware of my reaction, more settled, and calmer, what is possible here? What response is the most effective, skillful, and loving? What is my best choice under these circumstances?"

Can you think of a recent event that caused you distress for which you might use these tools?

This section has focused on developing a mindset and learning tools to improve your communication with others. Try choosing one person who matters to you, and think about how you might change the way you talk with them. To begin, choose someone with whom you feel safe. With some practice, you can then move forward in more important intimate relationships to take a risk and talk about more difficult issues.

Take that first step, and be more responsible for your own well-being and health.

Finding Your Spirit with Others

> **Lesson Learned from My Patients**
>
> When I am critical of others, my world gets smaller, and my choices seem more limited. A sense of gratitude fills me with comfort and helps me focus on what I have rather than on what is missing.

Increase Your Sense of Power

Cancer can be isolating and lonely and a challenging wake-up call. When you don't feel well physically, it's hard to see others living their lives while you feel at a standstill. Even though you might not always be able to plan too far ahead when you don't feel well, it is important to find the strength to believe and hope in a future that is not filled with pain and suffering to manage the isolation. We all take a lot for granted until we can't. Little things—seeing your child laughing, hearing the sounds of the birds in the morning, watching the sunset—can become a source of strength when other life choices seem limited.

Perhaps you can't physically do what you used to do before cancer. The challenge is, what can you do right now? What are the choices in front of you? Finding ways to make the present moment fuller, more meaningful, and more engaging can be a challenge for anyone. We all spend so much of our thinking in either the past or the future that we lose the power of living in the present moment. Finding someone or something to connect to right in front of you is a way to reduce the isolation. Identifying what you need now increases your sense of control when things are tough. Taking some control of what is possible now will help reduce your fear and anxiety. If you can identify what you need, then you can ask for it. For example, do you need to be alone when you feel poorly, or do you want someone there to support you? Please remember, no matter how much others care, they can't know what you want or need unless you tell them.

Couples often fall into the trap of assuming their partners either know or should know what they need. This type of thinking causes disappointment and frustration. No matter how long you have been in a relationship with someone, you must communicate what you want and feel. No mind reading allowed!

In her TEDx Talk "7 Notes on Life," Amy Rosenthal, who died in 2017 of ovarian cancer, expressed the importance of a focus on now and how you want to be now. Using the keys on the musical treble clef, she gave some powerful tools to help you live more fully in the now.

Tool: Play Your Own Song

- **A: Always** trust magic. Can you remember when events seem like a coincidence? You might have thought about someone or something, and the next thing you knew, you heard from that person, or something came up that answered your problem. This concept, introduced by Carl Jung, has been called synchronicity or meaningful coincidences. You can't figure out the cause of why it happened, but it seems meaningful.

- **B: Beckon** the lovely. What you focus on and look for determines not only your experience but also your mood. How about trying to open up to the possibility of something that brings you positive, loving energy?

- **C: Connected**. We are all connected. This does not mean by the internet or text but refers to feeling a sense of connection rather than isolation. This sense of connection is vital to health and well-being. Of course, you need alone time to recharge and revitalize, but too much isolation is not healthy for anyone.

- **D: Do**. Think, *What should I really be doing today?* Find the time to include what you know is the right thing for you today. Tell yourself that it is important, and don't let the external world get in the way. Be careful to keep your goal small enough to just begin. One step is the place to start.

- **E: Empty** space. As in music, the space between the notes is as important as the notes. The idea of regularly choosing to disconnect and just *Be Here Now* is golden and sacred. Opening up to the present provides the space for creation (reaction turned around).

- **F: Figure** it out as you go. You can't always know how things will turn out. As long as the edges are solid and you are operating from a place of truth and intention, just begin.

- **G: Go** to it. Tune into what makes you feel alive. Seek out what brings you energy and positive vibrations.

Find your song, and play it in your special key. Express yourself.

Different Strokes from Different Folks

What kind of strokes do you need from others? A support network can provide you a sense of security, belongingness, and acceptance. It can increase your confidence and feelings of competence and help you manage stress. This can include varying kinds and depths of relationships that suit your specific needs. Support means different things to each of you. What you need changes as your life changes. Although close friends might be part of your support network, I would like for you to think about some of the different ways in which others might support you at this challenging time in your life.

Look at the different ways you might need others and who in your life might be providing these needs. If a need is not being met, think about how, where, and with whom you might get this kind of support in the future.

Tool: Be Clear on the Support You Need

- *Intimacy.* Who in your life provides you with closeness, warmth, and acceptance and makes you feel free to express your feeling freely? Whom do you trust, and who is open to you?
- *Sharing.* Who shares your concerns and might be on the same journey? Who might you share information and ideas with and perhaps exchange favors with?
- *Self-worth.* Who respects your level of competence and understands the difficulty or value of the role you play as a worker, mother, and more and recognizes your skills?
- *Assistance.* Who provides needed resources to you, and whose help is not limited by time or the extent of their help? Whom can you depend on in a crisis?
- *Guidance.* Who provides you with advice and ways to solve problems? Who helps you take steps toward solving these problems to achieve your goals and take action?
- *Challenge.* Who in your world makes you think, questions your reasoning, and challenges you to grow?

You might not have specific people to meet each of these needs in your current support system. You might want to think about how and where you might find others to round out your support. Can you reach out to a cancer support group, an organization that is of interest to you, or a religious group that feels right to you? We all need others. How can you build a stronger support system to travel with you on your healing journey?

_____

_____

The Importance of Gratitude

Given all the losses my patients have endured, I have seen how cancer changes what becomes most important and relevant in their lives. Mary Pipher, PhD, in the January 12, 2019, issue of the *New York Times*, expressed this well: "Gratitude is not a virtue, but a survival skill, and our capacity for it grows with our suffering. That is why it is the least privileged, not the most, who excel in appreciating the smallest of offerings."

Robert A. Emmons, PhD, defines *gratitude* as an "affirmation of goodness." We affirm that there are good things in the world, including gifts and benefits we've received. Gratitude defines the source of this goodness outside you. Either other people or, if you believe, a higher power have given you these gifts, big or small, to help you achieve the goodness in your life.

One of the best ways to focus on gratitude is to start a gratitude journal in which you remind yourself of the gifts, grace, benefits, and good things you enjoy. Set aside some time at least once or twice a week to recall moments of gratitude associated with ordinary events, your personal strengths, or valued people in your life. When you are writing, pay attention to the aspects of your life that lead to feeling gratitude.

Tool: Writing Your Gratitude Journal

- Go for depth. Write more than just a list, and try to go into a little more detail about the aspects of your life you are grateful.
- Try subtraction, not just addition. One way to help identify sources of gratitude is to think about what your life would be like without certain blessings, rather than just adding up all the good things.

- Savor surprises. Try to record events that were unexpected or surprising, as this helps strengthen gratitude.
- See each item of gratitude as a gift. Be aware of your feelings, and savor and relish the gift in your imagination. Take your time in doing this; it's not just another thing on your to-do list.

Gratitude allows you to celebrate the present. It blocks toxic, negative emotions, such as envy, resentment, and regret. These emotions, although normal, are not good for your physical or emotional health. Grateful people have a higher sense of self-worth. Gratitude leads to a sense of abundance because you begin to realize that you already have so much of what you need. Gratitude is a gift you give yourself. It can help fill you up and help manage the feelings of loss that come from the struggle of cancer.

> You wander from room to room hunting for the diamond
> necklace that is already around your neck.

> —Rumi

> The person who has stopped being thankful has fallen asleep in life.

> —Robert Louis Stevenson

Can you give gratitude a bigger place in your life? Cultivating feelings of gratitude can enrich all of our lives. This feeling of fullness comes over me particularly when I am in nature. What brings you that sense of fullness?

Buy yourself a blank journal, and start it today. If you cannot see yourself writing in a journal, take a few moments each night before you go to bed to think about something you can feel grateful for that day in your life. The positive energy of these grateful feelings can bring you hope and harmony. What are you grateful for in your life?

_____

_____

The Value of Cultivating Compassion

The word *compassion*, derived from Latin, literally means "to suffer together." Although you can identify and empathize with others, compassion occurs when those feelings and thoughts include the desire to help. Your body produces oxytocin (tend-and-befriend hormone) when you feel compassion. When you help others, your brain also releases dopamine, which is like a reward itself. It is a gift to be able to give to others.

It is often difficult to know how to show compassion when someone is struggling. Most of the time, we feel the need to do something and feel inadequate in just listening to the pain of others. You have probably had caring people say things that were not at all helpful to you. People often forget that the most caring response can be to just listen. Deep listening provides an open, engaged space for the other person. You let yourself be emotionally touched so that the other can feel felt.

It is important to be mindful not to get overwhelmed yourself. Empathy without being mindful of your own reactions can cause pain. In trying to do or say something to make a situation better, others can feel rushed or cut off. You might have felt this when others tried to help you during your cancer.

Silence can be powerful. The gift of a caring, calm presence comes when you are calm and able to speak from your inner voice and the truth in your heart. Whether you are trying to show compassion to others or need to let others know what you need, try one of the tools below.

Tool: Compassion Tips

- "I am so sorry you are in pain" is a powerful, caring way to show love and concern.
- Try to keep your own anxiety in check. Take a moment to identify your own feelings before you speak. Consider putting your hand on your heart to help yourself identify your true compassion.
- "What is this like for you?" or "Do you feel like talking about your condition?" are open-ended questions that are caring.
- Your tone of voice matters.
- Don't offer advice unless asked.

- Your emotional sensitivity increases in the face of illness.
- Speak from your heart.
- Accept that the other person might not want to talk.
- It's OK if there are sadness and tears; just be kind to yourself and others. It is helpful to use your breath to calm and balance yourself when you have a painful reaction to another's suffering.

Below is the bodhisattva Prayer for Humanity by the sixth-century sage Shantideva. I believe it is relevant to all who wish to alleviate some of the suffering in the world.

> May I be medicine for those who are sick. May I be a resting place for those who are weary. May I be a lamp for those who are in darkness. May I be a bridge, a boat, and a raft for those to cross over the flood. May I be food for the hungry. May I be inspiration for those who are dispirited. And may I do so for as long as earth, and sky, and galaxies exist, so that all beings, I and all beings, are awakened together.

Lessons from Geese
Based on the work of Milton Olson
Dr. Robert McNeisch

In my workshops, I often show a movie that is a powerful example of how we all benefit when we work together: *The Ultra Geese*. This 1998 movie shows us what we can learn from geese. Once you read this, I bet you will never look at geese flying above you in the same way!

- **Fact 1:** As each goose flaps its wings, it creates uplift for the birds that follow. By flying in a V formation, a flock adds 71 percent greater flying range than if one goose flew alone.

  Lesson: People who share a common direction and sense of community can get where they are going easier and more quickly because they are traveling on the thrust of one another.

- **Fact 2:** When a goose falls out of formation, it suddenly feels the drag and resistance of flying alone. It quickly moves back into formation to take advantage of the lifting power of the bird immediately in front of it.

  Lesson: If we have as much sense as a goose, we stay in formation with those headed where we want to go. We are willing to accept their help and give our help to others.

- **Fact 3:** When the lead goose tires, it rotates back into formation, and another goose flies to the point position.

  Lesson: It pays to take turns doing the hard tasks and sharing leadership. As with geese, people are interdependent on each other's skills, capabilities, and unique arrangements of gifts, talents, or resources.

- **Fact 4:** The geese flying in formation honk to encourage those up front to keep up their speed.

  Lesson: We need to make sure our honking is encouraging. In groups where there is encouragement, the production is much greater. The power of encouragement (to stand by one's heart or core values and encourage the heart and core of others) is the quality of honking we seek.

- **Fact 5:** When a goose gets sick, wounded, or shot down, two geese drop out of formation and follow it down to help and protect it. They stay with it until it dies or is able to fly again. Then they launch out with another formation or catch up with the flock.

  Lesson: If we have as much sense as geese, we will stand by each other in difficult times as well as when we are strong.

As you move forward on your cancer journey, I hope you will realize that you cannot and should not travel alone. Although you can feel physically and emotionally isolated with your pain, connection to others is vital for your health. Your family, tribe, or community can walk with you as you lead the way to finding your right path. Take ownership for what you want, and find the courage and skills to communicate your needs. Others might disappoint you, but the opportunity to change requires you to take that first step. Consider taking action using these as examples to empower yourself and your relationships with those who matter to you.

Committed Action Contract

I will honestly think about my needs for physical intimacy and how I might build more acceptance of my body and how it has changed.

_____.

I will take responsibility for my part in the last disagreement and plan a time to discuss it with the other person.

_____.

I will take a few minutes either at the beginning of my day or at bedtime to identify what I am grateful for that day.

_____.

I will reach out to someone who can give me the kind of support I need to move forward with less fear and anxiety.

_____.

I will begin these changes by_____
(specific date).

_____.

Developing tools to feel more accepting of your body as well as gaining skills in communicating with others will build your strength to meet the challenges of cancer. Treating yourself with love and compassion will increase your inner strength and build a sense of gratitude that will fill your heart.

4

Focus on the Lane You Are In

Direct Your Energy

- Use your physical senses to bring the present alive.
- Direct your thoughts to build mindfulness.
- Develop your self-compassion to enhance your inner strength.

How you think about time changes after a cancer diagnosis. You might ask, "How long will treatment take? How long will I feel this sick? Will my life be shortened? When will things get back to normal?" When you feel ill, time can seem to drag, and each moment can seem endless. Good times can feel too infrequent or short.

The way you sense the passage of time is determined by how you think about what is happening to you. Worrying about what will happen, although normal, changes the present moment and your ability to truly experience what is occurring right in front of you. What is under your control is the now, not what might happen or what already has happened. In one of her videos, Loretta LaRoche says, "Yesterday is history. Tomorrow is a mystery. Today is a gift, which is why we call it the present." I also like the wise words of Bea Meltzer: "Yesterday is a canceled check. Tomorrow is a promissory note. Today is ready cash. Spend it wisely."

This chapter will provide you with tools to help you better experience the present moment. Although there is no guarantee each moment will be pleasant or positive, your attention to what is happening to you in the present moment will bring you a clearer focus and help you move forward.

We will talk about how your body can benefit from your changing your focus from time urgency to a more balanced sense of time. You will learn how you can challenge your self-defeating thoughts to live your life authentically. We will also discuss how being more present enlarges your spirit to bring a sense of abundance, letting go, and compassion.

So let's focus on the lane you are in.

Bring Your Body into the Present Moment

> **Lesson Learned from My Patients**
>
> There is never enough time when I fear that my life might be shortened or that I might lose some future opportunity. By my slowing down to the speed of now, time expands. This helps me live each moment more fully and have more clarity and space to know what I am truly feeling. I might not always feel at ease with the present moment, but I can use my awareness to better know what my next step can be.

As discussed in chapter 1, when you are stressed, your autonomic nervous system is aroused. Not only your body but also your thinking is affected by stress. It is believed the amygdala—that part of the brain associated with emotions and memory formation—is activated by noise and releases stress hormones. That is one reason why, when you are stressed, when you see your doctor, you might not clearly remember what they said. Each person has specific situations, people, and circumstances that create stress for them. As I said, stress is about any change that feels too much for you to handle. As much as it is impossible to completely avoid stress, finding some form of stress reduction can decrease the activity in your brain and increase your sense of well-being. Whether it is a break from the noise in your environment or from the chatter in your own mind, silence can be healing. Studies have shown that two minutes of silence can lower blood pressure and change brain circulation.

As I have said, your breath is the quickest and easiest way to slow down your nervous system. Dr. Andrew Weil is one of the leading voices for integrative medicine. His relaxing 4-7-8 breath (www.drweil.com) is a great way to let go of stress and focus on your body and letting go.

Tool: Relaxing Breath

1. Exhale completely through your mouth, making a whoosh sound.
2. Close your mouth, and inhale quietly through your nose to a mental count of four.
3. Hold your breath for a count of seven.
4. Exhale completely through your mouth, making a whoosh sound to a count of eight. This is one breath.
5. Now inhale again, and repeat the cycle three more times for a total of four breaths.

Don't worry about the exact time of each breath, but keep the counts at four, seven, and eight. This might help you get to sleep at night but can also be used whenever you are in a stressful situation. Before you begin any activity, take a minute to try this tool. (I use it all the time as a way to anchor and center myself.)

Time Urgency

Time urgency is the belief you do not have enough time to do what you need to do. With cancer, trying to find the time to manage treatments and appointments along with the daily demands of life can reinforce this belief. In general, however, we all function with this urgency. This kind of pressure creates stress both physically and emotionally. Get to know your body clock, and pay attention to your peak periods. When do you feel clearer and more focused and have more energy?

Tool: Slow to the Speed of Now

1. Decelerate. Eat, talk, and walk more slowly. Drive in the right lane more. How does your body feel when you are in the left lane as opposed to the right?
2. Treat delays (e.g., long lines and railroad crossings) as found time, and focus on more positive thoughts while you are waiting.
3. Modulate. When you can't cut back or slow down, vary your rhythm. Change positions often.
4. Choose to check or respond to your computer or phone less often. Create a schedule that feels less pressured for you, and be brave enough to follow it.
5. Create a ritual for a period of time when you cancel time and create a time of nondoing. (The Sabbath, for many religions, is a time for reflection, rest, and renewal.)

Look over this list. Which of these suggestions will you practice today to reduce your time urgency?

_____

_____

Your five senses provide critical information for your survival and warn you of danger. They also can be a source of pleasure and guide your well-being. Connecting to your physical senses helps you focus on what is presently happening to you. You are more in the present moment and more mindful.

Tool: Using Your Five Physical Senses

Touch

Your skin is your body's largest organ, with millions of nerve receptors. Many health care professionals have touched you in your cancer journey. There have surely been times when you felt physical pain. Although most have tried to be mindful of not hurting you, it is still important to speak up if you feel you are being touched in an uncaring, harsh manner. We all need to be touched in caring ways. It is basic for survival. To increase the positive benefits of touch, try the following:

- Give or get a hug or massage. You can even try self-massage: a gentle rubbing of your face, neck, or shoulders.
- Enjoy the weather, such as the wind on your face or the warmth of the sun.
- Walk on the grass or, if possible, stroll on the beach.
- Take a long bath or shower, and notice the feeling of the water on your body.
- Pet an animal.

Can you think of some other ways to increase positive touch in your life?

_____

_____

Sight

For many, sight is their dominant sense. We are all drawn to and seek beauty. Looking at nature can be healing for many. Consider the following:

- Focus on what is around you, and look outside whenever you can.
- Bring the outside in with a plant, a pet, or even a photograph.
- Look for color, texture, and shapes around you in nature.
- Really look into the eyes and face of someone you love.

When you raise your eyes from this page, what can you focus on that calms you?

_____

_____

Sound

We are seldom without sound around us. Often, silence is what we need as a refuge from both the noise of others or our own mental chatter. Sound affects your mood. Consider the following:

- Choose when you can listen to music that is healing for you. If right, music can bring you joy and calm, or if not right, it can frazzle you. (Isn't it amazing how the right music can trigger memories and the emotions you felt when you first heard that tune?)
- Seek sounds in nature that soothe and renew your spirit.
- Learn to play a musical instrument.
- Singing can change your energy level. (Don't forget to move to the music!)

Stop and listen to the sounds in your room, and bring your focus back to calming yourself.

Taste

Eating is a lot more than taste, yet how often do you truly taste what you are eating? Try the following:

- Eat more slowly.
- Taste with your nose, and smell your food.
- Pay attention to the colors of fresh fruits and vegetables.
- Try to bring variety into your meals.
- Try to decide when you are hungry or feeling some other emotion, such as boredom, exhaustion, or frustration. If it is not really food you need, try another sensual pleasure, such as listening to music, searching out others, or taking a walk.

The next time you eat, pay attention to each mouthful as you chew and swallow your food. Try to think about the source of where your food came from and the effort taken to grow or bring that food to your table.

Smell

There are more than ten thousand scents. Get to know your nose. Scents can trigger memories and be paired with healing behaviors. Aromatherapy is the ancient science of using different smells to create different moods. There are many essential oils you can choose to create a special scent. Scented candles are another way. Try the following:

- Practice relaxing, and associate a special scent with that feeling of calm and peace. Try using this scent at least six times to reinforce the fragrance in your odor memory.
- Identify the smells that create discomfort for you, and attempt to clean your environment of them and be proactive.

Try to find pleasant smells outside in the environment. What does freshness smell like to you?

_____

_____

Your Sixth Sense

Your intuition, your sixth sense, is the feeling you get in your gut when something does not feel right. Often, especially in times of stress, you don't pay attention to yourself or your feelings. I strongly believe this inner voice can help guide you during your cancer journey. Although I talk about challenging your negative thoughts to help yourself feel more empowered, it is also important to pay attention to that sense inside you when a situation feels off-center or wrong to you.

Along with available medical knowledge, using your intuition and inner awareness, you can be better prepared to increase your own healing. By developing your intuition, you improve your confidence in your decisions and your ability to problem-solve. Trust in yourself is important as you face the many decisions that cancer can demand in your daily life.

Suzanne was seeking a plastic surgeon for her reconstruction. She had educated herself on the different procedures and was scheduled to meet with a physician. The consultation went as planned, with the proposed procedure explained to her and her partner.

After the appointment, she felt unsettled. A nagging sensation in her stomach left her questioning if she would be comfortable having this surgeon operate on her. She questioned if she was just anxious about the surgery but decided to pay attention to her inner voice that told her she needed to find another surgeon.

She met with another physician, who recommended the same procedure; however, she felt a clearer sense of connection and safety with this surgeon. Trusting her intuition allowed her to approach her reconstruction with more confidence and trust in the outcome.

Tool: Build Your Sixth Sense

Pay attention to what your body is telling you. Your body is an intuitive antenna. When in doubt about an ache or pain, do not discount it; pay attention, and seek input from your physician if needed.

- Relaxation increases your ability to receive intuitive pictures, images, and symbols that your intuitive mind sends to you. When you have a gut feeling, can you slow down enough to allow an image to unfold in your mind's eye?
- Pay attention to your first impressions. Although they might need correction with more information, don't discount them outright without some consideration.
- Honor your hunches and flashes of awareness. Try to express your hunches concisely in a word or two. Your intuitive mind is brief and simple and responds without long discourse.

- Try to be aware of flashes or signals you have, ask yourself a question about them, and wait for a reply.
- Your intuition speaks in a quiet voice and will gently nudge you to respond.
- Be playful, and have fun trying to entice your intuition. Don't overanalyze and make it too serious.

Can you remember a time when you should have listened to your gut but didn't trust yourself enough to do what was in your best interest? How does it feel to continue to say no to yourself?

_____

_____

You need both instinct and reason to make the best decisions for yourself. There are many decision points on your cancer journey, and finding the balance of logic and instinct is not always easy. Whether you are committing to a treatment plan or deciding how to handle a difficult situation with someone, pay attention to both your inner voice and the voices of others and the information they give. The right answer for you might not be the same as the right answer for others. It takes courage and trust in yourself to honor the voice within you to move your healing forward. You might find journaling a good way to examine what you think and feel about a difficult issue.

Once you make a treatment decision, do not second-guess yourself. Take the time and effort to gather whatever information you need. When you decide, look forward, not backward. Do not undermine yourself. Remember, you are a unique individual, not just a statistic. Often, there is no one right answer to a challenging problem. Even if you need another opinion, there will come a point when you must make a decision. After you have sorted through the options, please try to trust your decision. Don't look back and doubt yourself, particularly when you have had to make a difficult treatment decision.

Which of the six senses will you focus on first to increase your ability to be in the present moment? Do you need to choose the sense you use less to create some small change in your daily life? Define how you will do this and when you can begin.

_____

_____

Bring Your Mind into the Present Moment

Lesson Learned from My Patients

Awareness has two wings: mindfulness and compassion. When I bring my awareness to seeing clearly what is happening now without judgment and open up to a tender, compassionate space inside myself, my life can move forward with more options.

We have all been told we must keep an open mind. What does that really mean? Usually, it is about being willing to think differently and look at another point of view.

Your thoughts are like a constant stream that fills the space between what is happening to you and your response to the situation. Thoughts automatically focus on either the past or the future and create emotions and sensations in your body. It is important to remember that you are more than your thoughts. By stepping back to investigate your thoughts about what is happening, you have the chance to respond rather than just react. We have limited control over what can happen in our lives. However, we can control the way we think about what has happened and the choices we make each and every day.

When you are stressed, your physical brain gets hijacked and overstimulated. Your ability to think clearly and make decisions is limited. Responding to others has much more power to effect change than just reacting.

So what can help you create some space between what is happening and the way you respond? The STOP tool once again can be a helpful reminder to come into the present moment.

Tool: The STOP Tool

STOP is a tool that is always available when you find yourself overreacting, stressed, or being mindless (mentally being somewhere else rather than where you really are). For example, where were you in your mind and thoughts when you were in the shower this morning? I bet you were physically there but mentally someplace different. That is what mindlessness is.

When you want to bring your attention to the present moment, imagine a stop sign:

> **S: Stop** what you are doing.
> **T: Take** a few breaths (doing so slows down the arousal).
> **O: Observe** your feelings and sensations.
> **P: Proceed** with what you need to do now.

Just the act of stopping and breathing causes a physical change in both your body and your brain. That space allows your brain to think clearly with more focus and attention. Your breath is the rhythm of your body and the way to shift your awareness to the present moment.

Mindfulness has become a buzzword for solving many of life's problems. The concept comes from Buddhist philosophy. A simple definition by Jon Kabat-Zinn, a pioneer in bringing mindfulness to Western medicine, is as follows: "Mindfulness is paying attention in the present moment without judgment."

Mindfulness is a tool that can help you observe your thoughts and create space to step outside those thoughts. It allows you to have more choice in how you respond. Mindfulness is an inner remote control to change the channel of your mind.

There are seldom any easy fixes for health and well-being. Mindfulness is a skill but not a ticket to happiness. With expanded awareness of the present moment, you may feel pain, joy, happiness, or sorrow. Over time, this awareness helps you to accept that life is never static and is always changing. Here are some key perspectives that can help build your ability to be in the present and better tune in to a more healing rhythm and connection to yourself.

Tool: Core Attitudes to Develop Mindfulness

- *Nonjudging.* Don't live by labels or categories. Try to see what is happening without labeling it as good, bad, terrible, or wonderful. Separate your opinions from the facts of who, what, where, or when it is happening. Even when you judge, don't judge your judging!
- *Patience.* Savor the moment with less rushing to the next moment. See and accept each moment, whether it feels like rain or sunshine.
- *Beginner's mind.* Look at what is happening as if for the first time, the way a child might view a new situation.
- *Trust.* Work to trust in yourself, your feelings, and your ability to learn and grow. It takes time to develop trust, and this is more of a challenge when life feels uncertain. Growing your ability to observe and be attentive will help build more trust in yourself.
- *Acceptance.* See things as they are in the present, and try not to always evaluate and judge.

Which of these attitudes might you focus on first to become more mindful?

_____

_____

As you can see, these are challenging attitudes to try to develop, and they require lifelong practice. Meditation is one of the more formal ways to develop your ability to be more mindful. It is a discipline that ideally is practiced on a daily basis. It does not require a belief in any particular spiritual or religious view. It can be looked at as a ritual that shifts the way you experience the moment. There are many misconceptions about what meditation is. Let's talk, though, about what meditation is not.

Meditation is not a way to stop thinking, because that is not really possible. It is an attempt to take a different relationship to your thoughts. When you focus on an object or your breath, you can observe without judgment your thoughts as they come and go. Quieting your mind is much more difficult than relaxing your body. Coming back to your focus can help you bring a sense of more balance between your mind and body. This is the beginning of being more mindful and in the present moment without judgment. You realize that your thoughts have a life of their own. You are more than your thoughts.

Meditation is not a form of self-help. It is not a fast route to becoming more emotionally calm or evolved than others. Letting go of the results when you practice is the aim. Meditation strives to help you stop trying to be someplace other than where you are at that moment. It is a spiritual practice but not a religious one. However, all types of prayer can be a form of meditation.

Meditation will not necessarily help you become more peaceful or content. It may, however, help you become more open, genuine, and gentle with yourself and others. Jon Kabat-Zinn stresses that you practice meditation for no reason and to get nowhere. The practice is to wake up and not miss the moments of life. Meditation is a more formal practice and tool to help you develop your ability to have an inner remote to change the channel of your mind. With regular visits to yourself, you can develop the power to observe your thoughts and create a space in your mind before you take action. Without attention, we tend to just repeat old patterns of behavior.

There are different forms of meditation, such as concentrating on your breath or on a word or phrase, such as a prayer. For many, religious prayer is a form of meditation. First, you must find a quiet place to take a seat. You do not have to sit on the floor cross-legged, but position yourself anywhere you can sit up fairly straight. Don't start by lying down, because you might fall asleep. The goal is to wake up so you do not miss the moments of life. You might find it helpful to find a community to support your meditation practice. There are many different sources of instruction. There are many resources available to learn and practice meditation online. One that some of patients have found useful is www.calm.com.

Tool: How to Develop Mindfulness Skills

Observe What Is Happening

- Notice what your experience is without reacting to it and getting caught up in it.
- Have a Teflon mind, and let experiences, feelings, and thoughts come into your mind and slip by.
- Control your attention, but see what is around you.
- Be alert to your feelings, thoughts, and actions.
- Watch how your thoughts come and go like clouds in the sky.
- Use your senses via your eyes, ears, nose, skin, and tongue.

Describe Your Experience

- Put words on your experience (e.g., "I am tight in my chest," "This sadness feels like a blanket over me," or "I have just thought that I can't do this.")
- Describe what is happening to you. Name your feeling. Call a thought just a thought or a feeling just a feeling.

Participate in Your Experience

- Try to get out of your head and into the experience of what is happening now.
- Use your intuition and wise mind to do what is needed in that particular situation.
- Practice these skills so you can change harmful situations and your unhealthy reactions to them and increase your acceptance of yourself and what life brings.

Can you think of one situation in which you might benefit from bringing these skills into action? Begin in a situation in which you are relaxed and can focus on these skills. Becoming more mindful is a lifelong practice and is not easy for any of us. Can you try to make one small step in developing these skills?

Can you commit even a few minutes each day to taking a seat and getting quiet enough to observe your thoughts? Allow whatever comes up to come up, and do not judge what is happening. There might be painful feelings, but trying to accept your experience allows you to begin to move forward to more self-care and awareness of what you need.

Tool: Everyday Mindfulness

Meditation is only one tool to increase your awareness of the present moment. There are many other ways to develop mindfulness in your daily life. It's important to remember to do just one thing at a time, whatever you are doing. Let go of distractions, and go back to what you are doing again and again. Some practical ways to increase your mindfulness are as follows:

Mindful Waking Up

- When you wake up, pay attention to your breath. Take a few deep breaths, and notice how you feel.

- Think of a positive image, or have a photo of one handy, and focus on it before you get out of bed.
- Notice what your thoughts are about the day, and remember that you can change your thinking.

Mindful Walking

- Notice when you are rushing, and pause to settle your energy and breathe more mindfully.
- Pay attention to your senses, particularly when you walk outside.
- Notice the movement of your feet and body and what your posture is while you are walking.
- Get up during your day, and walk to settle your mind. Focus on your breathing to reduce stress and tension.

The book *Peace Is Every Step* by Thich Nhat Hanh can offer you more perspective on mindfulness practices.

Mindful Eating

- Have some meals with less outside stimulation—no TV, phone, or computer.
- Chew more slowly to truly taste your food and feel its texture.
- Think about what went into the growing, harvesting, and transit of the food to your table to increase your appreciation of it.
- Value your body by choosing healthy food to nurture and care for it.

Mindful Conversation

- Say hello and goodbye to loved ones with awareness.
- Listen to others, especially children, with full attention and an open heart.
- Speak to others with awareness of your tone and manner.
- Focus on what works in a given situation, and avoid labeling things as fair or unfair or right or wrong.
- Play by the rules, and don't look to get even.

- Act as skillfully as you can to meet the needs of each particular situation.
- Keep your objectives in focus. What do you want to accomplish?
- Work to let go of anger and a sense of righteousness that will hurt you.

How can you begin to bring more mindful living into your daily life? Choose a specific way to be more aware and mindful, and practice it for a committed amount of time. Can you put into words how it changes your experience of that activity?

_____

_____

Bring Your Spirit into the Present Moment

Lessons Learned from My Patients

Finding ways to come home to myself and listening to my compassionate inner voice are the best ways to live authentically and with purpose. I do not have to be perfect to be worthy of self-love.

How has your view of yourself changed since your cancer diagnosis? Are you more critical of yourself and stuck on your limitations? Often, when we are challenged by life, we believe that to move forward, we must push ourselves to do better and achieve more. We think we will motivate ourselves if we just push a little harder with more determination. Does harsh criticism really motivate you or anyone to change?

The Necessity of Self-Compassion

I have found that most women have a much easier time feeling and showing compassion toward others than directing it toward themselves. Most of us have an inner critic. Although this voice can be a motivator to change and grow, it is often negative, harsh, and not the best way to make changes. It is wrong to assume that unless you are critical, you will not work hard enough, will not succeed, or will do less than you should. There is no redeeming value in harshness in most situations in life. To develop self-compassion, you must first be aware of how your critical self causes painful emotions, such as guilt or shame. Remember, we all are imperfect beings and make mistakes. Life is hard, and most of us do the best we know how given the circumstances we face. Recognize that you need kindness when dealing with the challenges of life and cancer. It might help you to ask yourself the following:

> What kinds of things do you criticize yourself about? (e.g., appearance, relationships, work, or parenting)?
>
> What words do you use when you make a mistake (e.g., insults or kind concern)?
>
> How do you feel inside when you are highly critical of yourself?
>
> When you notice something about yourself you do not like, do you feel cut off from others or more connected to others, who are also imperfect?

In trying to develop more self-compassion, it is helpful to imagine how someone else who cares about you would respond to you when you have done something wrong. What language would a wise and nurturing friend, parent, teacher, or mentor use to gently point out how your behavior is not productive? How might they encourage you to do something different? What is the most supportive message you can imagine them saying to you? How would you speak to others to support them when they were struggling?

Being kind and compassionate with yourself is not selfish or needy. During difficult times, you have probably reacted to others in ways that are less than adequate or right. It is easy to judge yourself harshly and move into blaming, shaming, and guilt. Although we all need to identify how we can improve our behavior and relationships, guilt and shame are not the ways to grow toward your better self and heal.

Kristen Neff, PhD, is a well-known researcher in the field of self-compassion. Now, you might think that the more self-esteem you have, the happier you will be. She helps us see that self-esteem is often a fair-weather friend because it is dependent on whether you see yourself as succeeding or failing. It is based on how you often compare yourself to others, which can easily lead to feeling you are not good enough. There is always someone who is more attractive, smarter, more successful, healthier, and so on. Self-compassion is not self-esteem. There is no comparison to others or evaluating how well you perform or how good you look. Self-compassion involves caring for yourself in both good and bad times. When you are stuck in criticizing yourself, you cannot focus on others or their needs. Self-compassion can be an important alternative when your self-esteem is lacking.

Tool: Ways to Practice Self-Compassion

- Be mindful, bring your awareness to what you are feeling, and accept that you are struggling. Try saying to yourself, "This is really hard for me." Be kind to yourself rather than harsh and judgmental.
- Try being a friend to yourself in the same way you might treat someone you care about. Be more supportive when you make a mistake or have a difficult time. Judgment causes suffering and isolation, neither of which you need.
- Touch is a direct way to bring loving, healing energy to yourself or others. You might bring your hand to your heart or bring your hands together in a gentle manner.
- Try expressing a soothing sound, such as "Ahh," and let the sound vibrate throughout your body.
- Pay attention to the words you speak to yourself when you make a mistake. Can you soften the inner critic and find a more compassionate way to think about what you have done?
- Remind yourself that you are not alone and that struggle is part of life. Accept that the human condition is imperfect. We all live imperfect lives. When you get caught up in thinking, *This should*

not be happening (even when it is), you cause yourself even more suffering. Understanding why you got cancer is never an easy question to answer. Blaming yourself will only create pain and frustration. Loss and difficult times are all part of the human condition. Your challenge is to try to stay connected to yourself and others rather than isolate and bring more suffering.

Working to develop a courageous presence says that you are willing to address the pain and still try to have an open heart. When you can calm your body and mind, you create an open space to respond rather than just react to difficulty. By being more self-accepting and compassionate, you can be less afraid of making mistakes and more willing to keep working toward the challenges you must face. Self-compassion has been called portable therapy. You can provide comfort and kindness to yourself when you most need it, anytime or anyplace.

In which areas of your life are you most judgmental toward yourself? Can you think of a way you might show yourself more self-compassion and be a better friend to yourself?

_____

_____

You might remember a special person in your life who challenged you to do better. More than likely, they were firm and had high standards but acted with some compassion and respect toward you. Can you show yourself more self-kindness? Be gentle with yourself, and recognize how much you share a common humanity and connection to others. You might not be able to do things the way you did before cancer, but letting go of the judgment and being more compassionate is an important step in healing.

Why is it so hard to show yourself self-compassion? Perhaps you believe it is self-pity or weakness to acknowledge your physical or emotional pain and loss. Maybe you fear if you are compassionate with yourself, you won't be motivated to move forward. Is it possible you believe it is selfish or self-centered to focus on yourself?

These self-limiting beliefs not only are inaccurate but also negatively affect your well-being. Your body produces oxytocin (tend-and-befriend hormone), which reduces cortisol (the stress hormone) when you direct compassion toward yourself or others. Your health can benefit from compassion.

Tara Brach, PhD, in *Radical Acceptance*, speaks of the trance of unworthiness. We are so judgmental of ourselves that often, we don't even realize it. How much do you tell yourself, "I'm not OK. I am not good enough"? Critical self-talk causes you to suffer and feel anxiety and fear. This not only is bad for your body but also erodes your self-worth, and you judge not only yourself but also others. You change through love, not judgment. Brach talks about using the RAIN tool to help you uproot painful beliefs. The first step is to take a U-turn to shift your attention from an outside focus of a person, a situation, or your thoughts to what is actually happening in your own body. This U-turn is the first step in tuning in to your negative self-talk so you can move forward with some compassion.

When you are feeling emotional pain—anxiety, fear, or sadness—sit; take a few deep breaths; and, if possible, relax any tension in your body.

Tool: Tara Brach's RAIN Tool

- *R: Recognize* what is happening. What emotions are you feeling? Where and how in your body does this emotion feel?
- *A: Allow* honestly what is occurring, and send yourself the message "Let it be." Although it might be tough, given the struggle or pain that is happening, tell yourself at this point in the process, "What is is. I am struggling."
- *I: Investigate*, and be curious as to what that hurt part of yourself needs with kindness. Can you identify any belief or thought that comes up and ask yourself, "What do you need from me?" What recognition, acceptance, forgiveness, or love does this suffering need? How can you bring kindness and compassion through words or actions?
- *N:* Try *not* to be identified or trapped in your hurt self. Breathe, and offer kindness to yourself the way a loving person would to a child. Recognize that you are more than your ever-changing thoughts. What words, touch, energy, or image might you bring to heal the wounds inside you?

Rachael, fifty years old, in the middle of her chemotherapy regimen, was having difficulty concentrating and focusing at work. She had always been a highly respected member of her team but was now unable to meet deadlines. With some self-reflection, she was able to say that she was fearful of losing her strong reputation as a team leader. She was struggling with fatigue and side effects and needed to reduce her responsibilities. She needed to be gentle with herself and accept her current limitations. In our session together, I asked her to close her eyes and remember a time when someone had been gentle and supportive of her when she was scared and vulnerable. She was able to see in her mind's eye her best friend hugging her after her miscarriage many years before. This loving image helped her to gain the courage to ask for a leave of absence.

Rachael's team was able to build a more cohesive unit in which others could grow professionally and develop new skills. Rachael returned to work with a greater appreciation of the role others could provide and recognized that she could give up some control and still be a valued team member.

Tara Brach also suggests you put your hand over your heart as you send loving-kindness to yourself. This RAIN tool can be helpful with both physical and emotional pain. By sending compassion and loving-kindness to yourself, you are better able to connect to the well of love inside you to help yourself heal and find the needed balance of mind, body, and spirit. As with many coping tools, this is not a quick fix. This tool is one that will take many times to practice to create a pathway for self-compassion inside you. You are worth the time!

Let's look at the various paths to bring compassion into your daily life.

Tool: Pathways to Self-Compassion

- *Physical:* Care for your body, and create no harm. Is there one small change you can make to value your body with more care?
- *Mental:* Allow your thoughts to arise without judgment. You will not always have kind, loving thoughts. Can you be more accepting of yourself when you make a mistake?
- *Emotional:* Accept your feelings, no matter what they are. There will be times when you are angry or not at your best with others. Try not to deny your limitations.

- *Relational:* Connect authentically with others. Be real, even if you are not perfect.
- *Spiritual:* Nurture your values. Try to live in alignment with what is truly important to you.

Can you choose one of these pathways to increase your self-compassion and identify a small change you can make today? The road to self-compassion is a winding one, but will you start with just one small step?

_____

_____

How self-compassionate are you?

Tool: How You React to Yourself

- What types of things do you typically judge and criticize yourself for (e.g., appearance, career, relationships, or parenting)?
- What type of language do you use with yourself when you notice a flaw or make a mistake (do you insult yourself, or do you take a kinder and more understanding tone)?
- When you are being highly self-critical, how does it make you feel inside?
- When you notice something about yourself you don't like, do you cut yourself off or reach out to connect with others, who are also imperfect?
- What are the consequences of being so hard on yourself? Does it make you happier and more motivated or discouraged and depressed?
- How do you think you would feel if you could truly love and accept yourself exactly as you are? Does this possibility scare you, give you hope, or both?

Can you remember a time when you were being critical of yourself?

Try to use the above questions to explore how you might treat yourself with more compassion.

_____

_____

Tool: How You React to Life Situations

- How do you treat yourself when you run into challenges in your life? Do you tend to ignore the fact that you're suffering and focus exclusively on fixing the problem, or do you stop to give yourself care and comfort?
- Do you tend to get carried away by the drama of the situation and make a bigger deal out of it than you need to, or do you tend to keep things in balanced perspective?
- Do you isolate yourself from others when things go wrong, with the irrational feeling that everyone else is having a better time of it than you are? Do you get in touch with the fact that everyone faces hardship in their life?

If you feel you lack sufficient self-compassion, check in with yourself. Are you criticizing yourself for this too? If so, stop right there. Try to feel compassion for how difficult it is to manage serious illness and continue to live up to the external standards set in our society. Trying your best to heal is enough of a challenge. You don't need to be perfect to be worthy of love. Practicing self-compassion is the place to begin.

Tool: A Buddhist Way to Build Self-Compassion

Sharon Salzberg, PhD, a well-known Buddhist teacher, in *Loving-Kindness: The Revolutionary Art of Happiness* (2002), has some helpful suggestions for how to practice self-compassion.

1. Spend some time reflecting on a quality you possess that is good and helpful to others. (Are you a good listener or a kind friend?)
2. When you judge anger or fear as a feeling that is bad or weak, try using the word *pain* or *suffering* to describe your reaction. (How does this change the feeling of judgment?)
3. Practice some form of self-care for fifteen to twenty minutes per day to be kind to yourself.
4. Find the gray in a situation or relationship rather than a black-and-white judgment. (As hard as it is, most things in life are not that clear-cut.)
5. Practice a loving-kindness meditation.

Loving-kindness meditations are based on the belief that we are all connected with others and their sorrow because we are all interconnected. I know you have sat in your doctor's office and felt a different kind of connection to those around you because you know their pain in a physical way that others without cancer have not experienced. This feeling might feel raw and vulnerable, especially when you see other patients' cancer progress. Perhaps when you allow yourself to feel a sense of love and wholeness within you, the world has a nucleus of love and kindness that it lacked a moment before. This can benefit you and others.

Tool: Loving-Kindness

1. Find a quiet place where you will not be interrupted.
2. Focus on your breathing, and watch the rising and falling of your chest and belly.
3. Create a clearing of softening and opening, and bring to your mind a feeling of warmth and love that you feel or have felt from someone else.
4. When your thoughts come up (and they will), allow them to come and go like waves of the ocean—always moving, rising, and falling.
5. When you feel calm, repeat the following to yourself:
   May I live in safety.
   May I have peace and joy.

> *May I have health and freedom from pain.*
> *May I live with ease.*

You may also want to direct these words to others. Allow them to flow from your heart, and when you lose focus, be gentle with yourself. There is no perfect way to practice this. Remember, judgment is what you are trying to move away from. We change through love, not judgment.

Self-compassion does not make your life easier or change what is happening, but it helps you feel stronger as you manage the challenge. Difficult challenges are like potholes in the road that must be filled with compassion.

I often use the image of a bank when I talk about the need to value and nurture yourself. If you want to have some money in your bank to withdraw, you must make some deposits. If not, you will be overdrawn and unable to give to yourself or others.

Try this loving-kindness practice. If you can focus for only a few minutes, begin there. Try this each day at a specific time (perhaps when waking or going to sleep) for at least a week. If it is too difficult to direct these loving thoughts toward yourself, start by directing them toward others you love.

Finding Refuge in the Present Moment

We all need a safe place to retreat to, either physically or in our mind's eye. This refuge can be seen as an escape, although it does not have to be viewed as avoiding what you need to do or achieve. Consider this quote from thirteenth-century Persian poet Rumi: "Do you make regular visits to yourself?" This is not meant to imply you should think only about yourself. However, can you imagine how you might grow and heal if you found a place of compassion and inner resource within yourself?

You might begin by saying to yourself, "I take refuge in …" If you can't decide, search for a memory when you felt safe, nurtured, or cared for in a way that lifted your mood or inspired you. (Perhaps it is a memory of a place in nature, an event, or someone you value.)

When you have this image, take a few minutes to identify where you feel this sense of safety in your body. Do you feel warmth, expansion, light, or some other physical sense? Breathe into this sensation, and let the feeling sink into you. Make sure you give yourself enough time to let this feeling nourish and fill you emotionally.

Although we can't prevent tough times, this skill of finding refuge or a safe place within yourself can help you manage your challenges with more inner strength.

Try this in the morning before you get out of bed to set the tone for the day. It might also help you prepare for sleep.

Dr. Paul Pearsall (1941–2007) was a neuropsychologist who lived in Hawaii and was a bright light in the field of psychoneuroimmunology (PNI), the science of how your mind and emotions affect your immune system. Although this interaction of the mind and body is complicated, we continue to learn more about its role in healing. His book is based on aloha, the Hawaiian philosophy of patience, unity, agreeableness, humbleness, and kindness. He speaks of healing as a journey and of the tools you need as the navigator on your voyage. You live by your five senses: sight, smell, taste, touch, and hearing. Your sixth sense, which reads energy you cannot always describe or measure, is also important to keep you safe and avoid things that threaten your survival.

Pearsall talked about a seventh sense composed of all the basic senses. It directs the other senses to detect what is true healthy pleasure. It is subtle and gets your attention by helping you focus on what is missing for a meaningful and enjoyable life. This seventh sense is food for your soul. The principles of aloha are the key to discovering and developing this sense. His tool to find the positive energy of aloha is as follows.

Tool: The SAFE Tool

S: Sit
A: And
F: Feel
E: Everything

First, you must stop physically and mentally moving. Once a day, find a quiet place with as many living things around you as possible—grass, trees, plants, pets, and so on. Next, stop doing and thinking, and try to just feel. There are no goals or agenda for this. Listen to the sounds around you, and feel everything and anything. Don't be selective. Free yourself for at least a few moments to just be with the world. This is not a meditation you have to do alone. Allow yourself to be enchanted by the simple things of life, the breath of life inside you, and the energy around you. Think during your safe time about those you love and have loved. Feel the connection, and reawaken to the fact that the gift of life is yours to waste or celebrate.

This SAFE tool is part of developing your ability to find balance and healing. Healing is a process, not a set destination. When life is difficult, Dr. Pearsall has some important suggestions for your healing.

- *Patient healing.* Healing can't be rushed. Give yourself the time you need to accept that life is as difficult as it is wonderful. Try to remember a good time to help bring the stored joy into the present. It won't take away the hard times, but the energy will help you through the challenges.
- *Harmonious healing.* Healing requires achieving harmony with others and restoring balance. Try to reach out rather than withdrawing into yourself. There will be times when you are in a dark place. Accept that this is part of the process, but recognize that light can follow darkness, and darkness brings light.
- *Pleasant healing.* You need people to help you heal. When you are suffering, you might drive others away when you need them most. Get in touch with your anger, and work to own it and find a path toward forgiveness. Forgiveness is not forgetting. You might decide you do not want further contact with those who anger you. You forgive for yourself, not for others.
- *Humble healing.* Time does not heal all wounds. Accepting what you can change and trying to let go of what you can't is an ongoing part of the healing process. Having some spiritual practice can be part of finding a balance. The power of prayer has been researched by Western medicine. One study showed that prayers for hospitalized patients by individuals who did not know the patient improved the course of their illness. Regular participation in organized religious activities has been shown to improve health in other studies (Koenig 2001). Any way you can connect to your source of higher power and light is a way to center and ground

yourself. Everyday spirituality includes reflecting on what brings you a sense of awe and meaning. Spirituality, in this sense, is different from religion, yet connection to a religious community might be a source of strength and healing for you.

- *Tender healing.* In our Western culture, we focus on doing rather than being. Illness, although never wanted, can offer an opportunity to enter into a gentler way of being. Try to open yourself to learning how and where you need to reconnect. Be kind to yourself, and take the time to pause and use the SAFE tool to navigate the rough waters of any loss.

Will you schedule a time today to use the SAFE tool?

I have tried to provide you with different tools to help you focus on the lane you are in. Being present and mindful of what is happening in your body can feel scary if you are managing physical pain and the uncertainty of illness. Whatever the source of your pain, you play a role in managing it by being able to communicate to the best of your ability what you are experiencing in your body. In order to do so clearly, you must be tuned in to the sensations, even when you are unsure why you feel that way. Pain, which is as individual as each person, constantly changes from moment to moment as you experience it. Knowing the internal thoughts you are having in your head also plays a role in how you respond to pain and other situations. Telling yourself, "I can't handle this," will throw you into more fear. Being mindful and aware of the words in your head allows you to refocus.

Consider how moving back to regulate and center yourself can give you a greater sense of internal control. Remember, you are more than your thoughts. You may not always have control over what is happening, but you can have some control and choice about how you think about what is happening to you.

Being able to self-regulate during difficult times is a valuable tool in managing illness. We all get caught up in anxiety, fear, anger, and stress. Being able to reduce the negative effects on your body requires a self-regulation practice.

Tool: Terry Fralich's Self-Regulation Practice

1. Tune in to your breath. Bring your attention to the exhalation and the softening quality of a relaxing breath (like a sigh).
2. Focus on the mind-body connection. Pick a word or phrase, such as "Relax," "Let go," or "Slow down." Silently repeat the word or phrase as you connect with your exhalation.
3. Use your imagination. As you connect with your exhalation while repeating your word or phrase, imagine your body softening and your energy settling.
4. Use positive visualization. Select an unconditionally positive memory, landscape, or image. Strengthen your connection with it by sharpening your internal view of it. See it in your mind's eye as fully as you can. Use the image to shift and settle your negative energy.
5. Choose a short phrase that creates peace for you. It may be a blessing, affirmation, intention, or prayer. Memorize it, and recite it when negative energy arises. This is your personal protector for your mind and heart.

Practicing mindfulness can be compared to learning the scales on a piano. It is a way to get the basics to play the music of your thoughts. Having a greater awareness of your body and the way you respond and think allows you to feel some choice. The best time to learn any new skill is when you are not in a crisis. It's like having GPS coordinates to guide you on your road trip and help you manage the route. Although we are never totally prepared for what will happen, the control we have is in the present moment. It's not "what if" but "what now."

Mindfulness is a life skill and must be practiced. Coming to this practice with an attitude of compassion will help you move forward in your healing journey. Mindfulness helps you live with more choice rather than just out of habit. Connecting to the power inside you allows you to respond with more calm, wisdom, and vitality.

Mindful transitions are a good way to settle stressful energy during the day. Take a few seconds several times a day (or as often as you want) to create a mindful transition. Link this mindful-transition practice with a repeating activity you do during the day. For example, when you walk to the car, wait for a doctor's appointment, or go to the bathroom, stop and bring these core skills into your daily life.

Tool: Steps to Create Mindful Transitions during Your Day

1. Stabilize your attention. Bring your attention to your softening breath.
2. Cultivate the witness. Check in with the state of your mind, emotions, and body.
3. Practice self-regulation. Relax, and soften your body.
4. Practice loving-kindness. Be patient and gentle with the state of your being, even if you wish it were different.

Think of an activity you do every day, and link it with a mindful transition using the above skills. For example, use each time you wash your hands as an opportunity to direct some compassionate kindness toward yourself or others. Commit to doing this for at least a week. What do you notice?

_____

_____

We began this chapter by talking about time. The concept of time is central to mindfulness. I saw a post about imagining time as money. It suggested you look at the seconds of each day as $86,400 in your bank account. The money goes away at the end of each day and is replaced the next day. How do you want to spend your money in your life account?

Practical mindfulness helps you focus and make choices about what is really important to you. Spending your time with more awareness increases the value of each moment. It is not a guarantee that each moment will be easy but is a way to spend those moments with greater awareness, intention, and empowerment in your healing journey. Committing to change requires specific, realistic, measureable goals you can write down. Consider this sample as a way to begin.

Committed Action Contract

I will take time at least once a day to stop what I am doing and tune in to what I am feeling in my body as a way to respond with more awareness of what I need.

I will create a way to wait for appointments so that it will be my special time to relax.

I will challenge one critical thought about how my body has changed with a more compassionate understanding of how difficult managing cancer can be for anyone.

I will begin these changes by_____(specific date).

Be where you are. Otherwise you will miss your life.

—Buddha

This chapter has provided tools to help you better connect to your physical sensations and inner voice. Mindfulness is a daily practice that requires a commitment to face and allow yourself to experience what is happening to you now. When life is difficult, self-compassion and kindness can ease the pain and grow your love for yourself and others.

5

Navigating the Exit Ramp

Facing the Fear of Death

- Communicate the care you want.
- Become aware of what truly matters to you.
- Maintain hope to weather the roadblocks.

> **Lessons Learned from My Patients**
> Serious illness forces me to face my fear of death long before I feel ready to do so. Life is not fair, and people do not get what they deserve. Bad things happen to good people. I must learn to accept difficult and unfair situations and find a way to create peace within myself.

Some of you will not want to read this chapter and will think I have made a poor decision to include it in a book focused on tools for coping with cancer. I, however, believe it would be a major omission not to shine a light on death and focus on how you might want to navigate the challenging road at the end of life.

Death is not failure. Although none of us is ever completely ready to let go of someone we love or, even more so, our own life, we all know that life is finite. When you were first told of your cancer, fears about death were right in front of your face. The intensity of this fear fades more into the background with the passage of time and good health. In my work with patients at all stages of the cancer journey, I have seen how fear

139

continues to resurface. A scan, a symptom, or an unusual new pain can create uncertainty and worry about how fragile your health feels. As I said earlier, breast cancer has become more of a chronic disease than a death sentence. The latest statistics (2020) state that 3.5 million women either have a history of being treated or have finished treatment in the United States. Although the death rate continues to drop, 42,170 women are expected to die in 2020 from breast cancer (www.cancer.gov).

Susan Gruber, a cancer survivor, quoted Christopher Hitchens in the July 25, 2019, issue of the *New York Times*: "As you struggle to survive in the present, you simultaneously imagine your demise." The incredible challenge of cancer is the balancing act of living your life with all the uncertainty and possibility of death.

We are a society that wants to avoid talking about death and believes it is morbid and pessimistic to even think about dying. Beneath the anxiety and uncertainty of cancer is this unspoken issue: death. Although we all know the death rate remains 100 percent for us all, few patients are willing to talk directly about it. Many of my patients fear others will become uncomfortable or think it means they have given up trying to live if they discuss death. There is a tombstone in Ashby, Massachusetts, that reads, "Remember, friend, as you pass by, as you are now, so once was I. As I am now, so you must be. Prepare yourself to follow me."

Many people look at death as the enemy. Medicine and doctors focus on finding a physical cure and doing everything possible to fight the disease. Doctors can find it difficult to directly discuss death with their patients, as they might see it as a failure of their ability to do their job well. Each of you reading this book is at a different phase in your cancer treatment and journey. Most of you are focused on how you want to manage treatment, get physically stronger, and bounce back into a renewed life. I hope this guide provides you with tools that enable you to do just that.

Some of you might have just had a reoccurrence or been told your treatment has stopped being effective. Your limited options might create fear that your life will be shortened. Whether you are living with cancer or know others who are, we all must face that death is a part of life. We cannot control all aspects of our lives or deaths, but we can play a role in how our final chapter is written and how our exit ramp is navigated.

As I said earlier, most of my patients continue to live full and active lives. The privilege of traveling along the road with those who have died has been meaningful, powerful, and sad. Each death has been as unique as each woman. My most personal journey was with a special friend who died of breast cancer fifteen years ago after a five-year struggle. She was very independent and often would not allow me to help her when she was in the terminal stages of her disease. I would become frustrated and concerned because she lived alone. I tried to fix things, especially when I was anxious about her physical limitations.

During her treatment, she worked with a therapist to help her to understand her old hurts and disappointments. Her dying process was her opportunity to examine unfinished relationships, especially a difficult divorce. The way she directly faced her death continues to be an inspiration for me. She tried to prepare those around her while attempting to emotionally accept the inevitable. She spent time with her only child, going through possessions and memories to help him cope better with the loss. I do not know if she was absolutely ready to die, but I often remember a time when we were together at the beach before she was too ill. We had just seen a beautiful sunset, and she said, "This can be enough." I think of her often when I am on that same deck, watching the sunset. I carry her presence and the grace of that moment within me.

Do I believe there is a right way to die? Certainly not, but I do believe that acknowledging death can cause us to live more fully and with more joy because we recognize our time is limited. Sometimes I think my awareness of the fragility of life has been influenced by my work with cancer patients and pushed me to try to live my life with more focus. Questions about what brings meaning and purpose to my life always surface when I face my mortality. Certainly, the loss of important people in my life has molded who I am. One cannot be a therapist without being able to confront loss in all areas of life. Death and loss are part of life. How we try to manage and deal with loss is up to each of us. I often say, "Death ends a life. Death doesn't end a relationship."

This chapter is my attempt to bring death out of the closet so you can begin to address issues that I believe will empower you. Although what you want and need changes as your life evolves, identifying what really matters to you can strengthen your personal power to live more fully. This chapter might also help you as you navigate the challenges of someone you love who may be facing a serious, life-threatening illness or challenge.

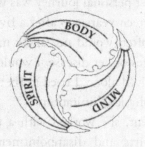

Identify Your Physical Needs

> **Lessons Learned from My Patients**
>
> It is a gift to those you love to tell them what you need and want before you are physically or mentally unable to do so. Others do not know what you need unless you tell them.

When most of us think about death, we fear physical pain. Although we are seldom ever ready to die, most are more afraid of pain and suffering than of death. Death is fundamentally a personal experience, but I believe that no one should have to die in pain or die alone. The COVID-19 pandemic that began in 2020 revealed the trauma of individuals having to face death alone without loved ones allowed to physically be with them. Realizing the uncertainty of life, we all feel the vulnerability of illness. As much as we cannot control all aspects of our dying process, we can play an active role with proper education and planning. This requires that you face the reality of what the medical system can provide and what you do or do not want for yourself.

My life experience around facing death was greatly affected by the fact that both my parents died suddenly. I had no chance to say goodbye or even know what was important to them in terms of end-of-life care. I have seen the emotional pain and damage that can occur when families are pulled apart by wanting different care for a loved one who is dying. Everyone has their own opinion about what should be done to either prolong or shorten life. If others do not know what you want, you leave them in a vulnerable position to try to figure out what you want. It is our responsibility to let others know our wishes about end-of-life issues.

Ellen Goodman, the founder of the online resource the Conversation Project, has said, "This conversation is one we want to avoid because it always feels too soon until it is too late." Ninety percent of us say that talking about end of life with loved ones is important, but only 27 percent have done so. Eighty percent of people say that if seriously ill, they would want to talk to their doctors about end-of-life care, but only 7 percent have had this conversation with their doctors.

Most of us feel we don't even know how to begin to discuss this difficult issue. The Conversation Project is a wonderful resource to help you begin. They have a starter kit that will work you through some of the important questions and how to begin, including the following:

- How long do you want medical care?
- Whom do you want involved in your care, and to what degree?
- What are the three most important things you want others to know about your end-of-life wishes?

When loved ones are facing terminal illness, there are many different kinds of conversations you should consider having, either for yourself or for a loved one.

Tool: What Conversation Might Work for You?

- Conversations about love involve telling others how much they matter.
- Identity messages involve a dying person telling survivors important thoughts that may influence who they are or might become.
- Religious or spiritual talks include times when you might read the Bible or other religious texts, recite prayers, or discuss thoughts about the afterlife.
- Everyday talk—spending time with each other when someone is dying—sends the message "I am living with you up until the moment you die."

- Difficult relationship talks may be an attempt to repair a hurt; however, these are not always possible.
- Specific logistical talks about wishes for end of life and funeral and burial plans can help people stop denying the reality of the situation.

Can you imagine how you might have one of these conversations? Whom in your life would you feel the safest with in communicating your needs and desires? You do not need to be terminally ill to begin one of these conversations.

_____

_____

Clearly, your decisions and priorities change as your life and health change. It is vital for everyone to begin this conversation. Even if you avoid the discussion, your loved ones need to know what you want. Otherwise, they are put in a position to make decisions on their own, deal with possible conflicts between family members, or feel guilty about the decisions they have made during a time of uncertainty.

This conversation is not just for the old, sick, or frail. It is for everyone: young adults, young parents, middle-aged people, and the geriatric and elderly population. It has been called estate planning for the heart. We all know that life might be cut short with little notice. The uncertainty and vulnerability bring home our mortality. We might not be totally clear about what we want in a life-or-death situation, but exploring what is important to you can empower you and provide some guidance to those who love you.

You might wonder when the best time to have this conversation is. Clearly, you, as the patient, must be ready to think about death and what is important to you. Although many fear death when first diagnosed, it takes time to directly face the possibility. For many, the right time is when treatments have failed to control the disease and one's body is too weakened to continue to function. Perhaps the catalyst for the conversation is seeing someone you know and love die and wanting your death to be different. Please remember that accepting death is not giving up. You want to be physically able to express and understand your options with an open mind and heart.

Tools: How to Begin the Conversation

These suggestions may help you in speaking to those you love about your personal needs or give you some guidance on how to be with others who might be near the end of their lives.

- Start early. Don't wait until time is too short and emotions are too fragile.
- Write it down. It's easier to speak when you have some idea of what you want to say in these difficult situations.
- Start with an explanation. Acknowledge that this talk is difficult, perhaps there is not much time left, and you want to make sure you say what you need while you can.
- Keep it brief. When people are sick, they have less emotional and physical energy. Pick one or two important things you want to say.
- Don't push religion. Not everyone has the same beliefs. Pushing your agenda might discount who they are.
- Keep your expectations small. Don't expect others to behave in a way that is out of the usual for them, especially when they are seriously ill.
- Be compassionate. In some situations, just staying silent or being forgiving is the greatest gift you can offer. Your greatest gift can be just being present.
- Be present. Sometimes the best talks happen when you least expect it. The more time you spend with a dying person, the more opportunities you might have.

On the Conversation Project website, there are even games to play together if you think that approach will work better for you or your loved ones. For example, the card game My Gift of Grace has questions for anyone to consider about living and dying well. The activities, from identifying your earliest memory of a difficult decision to writing your own epitaph in five words or fewer, can provide a means of discussing challenging topics.

Another organization, formed in 2013, Death Over Dinner, helps you plan a dinner. You might think this sounds unusual, but these dinners are happening all over the world. The dinner might include friends, family, or coworkers who come together with some preplanned readings or videos to begin the discussion about death. How many important discussions happen over the dinner table? These dinners are not meant to be morbid but stimulating and thought-provoking. You have a chance to hear others' experiences, think about your own, and define what is important to you. You only die once. How do you want to orchestrate what you can with this important event in your life?

Tool: Your Five Wishes

A simple way to begin to think about what is important to you is through the five wishes (www.fivewishes.org). These are as follows:

1. Who do you want to make health care decisions for you when you can't make them?
2. What kind of medical treatment do you want or not want?
3. How comfortable do you want to be?
4. How do you want people to treat you?
5. What do you want your loved ones to know?

Educating yourself is the most direct way to reduce the powerful vulnerability you feel around death. There are many resources available, such as podcasts hosted by a physician with End-of-Life University, to help you learn which questions to ask. For example, do you know the difference between hospice and palliative care?

Palliative care is medical care that may be available to you at any age, stage of illness, or treatment. It focuses on the whole person and addresses the mind, body, and spirit of the patient. You do not have to be in an active dying stage to get the support and assistance you need if this is available in your community.

The requirement of hospice care is more specific for those at end of life who have a prognosis of six months or less to live. Hospice programs focus on quality of life and symptom management when the patient is no longer receiving curative treatment.

YOUR JOURNEY BEYOND BREAST CANCER

It is important for you to either educate yourself on the services provided by your particular insurance company or enlist the help of your support system and medical team to get the information when it is needed.

There are many resources to help you manage some of the legal aspects of advanced directives as well as living wills. The important point is to address these issues when you have the time and emotional ability to sort out your choices. It is a gift of the heart to those you love. Consider visiting the following websites: Advance Care Planning Decisions (www.acpdecisions. org) and National Healthcare Decisions Day (www.nhdd.org). In addition, POLST.org is a resource for your physician to complete, listing specific medical interventions you may or may not want provided to you. This is more specific than an advanced directive or do-not-resituate (DNR) document.

As I write this guide, the world is continuing to cope with a worldwide pandemic. Both young and old are facing the realization of our mortality. With this awareness, end-of-life planning is an important topic. Websites that provide resources address the legal, medical, and emotional aspects of the dying and grief processes. The death positive movement is focused on the belief that talking about death empowers you to play a more active role in this final stage of your life. There are ways to connect with others in death salons online or train to become a death doula. Just as doulas assist women during the birth of children, trained individuals can play a supportive and therapeutic role at the end of life. Thinking about your needs when you can communicate will empower you to control the process as best you can. We all spend a great deal of time thinking about planning events in the future. This is one event we all will attend. How do you want to participate?

Thinking about dying can bring up fear and anxiety in us. However, thinking about what really matters to you will not mean you are not fighting hard enough to get better or are being overly pessimistic and negative. Acknowledging your mortality is an act of courage.

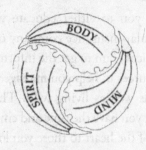

Identify Your Emotional Needs

> ### Lessons Learned from My Patients
>
> Pain is inevitable, but suffering is optional. I might not always avoid physical pain, but how powerless I feel is within my control. We all fear physical pain when we are vulnerable and ill. Having some tools to calm my body, adjust my thinking, and identify and communicate what I need will empower me to fear less.

All pain is real. Physical pain is like a conversation between the brain and the body. Like verbal conversations, it can be heated or calm. A sense of increased emotional safety can ease pain and loosen its grip. I am not saying you can think pain away, but how you manage your thoughts about what is happening to you can adjust your experience of pain and help you feel a greater sense of strength. I believe that many are more fearful of the process of dying than of death. Even with advances in medical science and medication, there can still be physical pain. Again, the importance of your communicating when you are able to do so can play a role in how your treatment is delivered. Suffering is painful but is as much an emotional process as a physical one. When medical options are limited, how you are able to let go and move toward acceptance of death can help ease the pain of your loss for yourself and those you love. Of course, how you die is as individual as how you live. Cancer forces you to recognize the fragility of life and the reality of your mortality.

Elisabeth Kübler-Ross, MD, author of *On Death and Dying*, was a pioneer in the field of death and dying. She wrote about the five stages of grief that help us understand any significant loss. Cancer is a loss and forces you to find a new balance. These stages of grief are not linear; you may or may not experience all of them or go through them in any specific order. The stages are responses to feelings that can last for minutes or hours as you move from one stage forward or backward. As you look over these stages, think about where you might be in your cancer journey.

Tool: Where Are You in Your Grieving Process?

The first stage of grief is denial. Perhaps when you first received your diagnosis, your initial reaction was *This can't be happening to me*. The shock of this trauma creates a sense of unreality and numbness. This is the normal response of your mind and body to protect you from the emotional pain of this loss. You probably did not hear anything else after the word *cancer*. This first-wave numb response allows you to have some space to begin to manage the challenges ahead. As denial fades, the need to cope with the feelings of fear begins.

The next emotional stage that might follow for some is anger. You might have felt angry during your journey. You might have asked, "Why has this happened to me?" Finding blame is one way to manage pain; however, staying stuck in blaming does not help you heal. You might question and blame God for your loss and lose your sense of faith. Anger is energy, but sorting out how to direct it and not turn it toward yourself is vital for your healing.

The third stage, bargaining, takes the form of a truce. *If only I could have taken better care, perhaps I would not have gotten cancer.* This mindset creates guilt and punishes the victim. You might have also thought that if only you had found the tumor earlier or been more aware of your health, you would not have gotten cancer. This mindset keeps you in the past, leaving you with less energy to focus on what is needed now. Remember, it's not "what if" but "what now." Focusing on the present allows you to take charge of what is needed to heal.

Depression is the next difficult but necessary stage of grieving. We mourn whatever we have lost that we value and love. In chapter 2, we talked about the difference between grief and clinical depression. Although grief and sadness are painful, you must allow these emotions to have some space to flow. Stuffing your sadness takes energy that, when freed up, gives you more emotional space to move forward.

The fifth stage, acceptance, does not mean you are OK with having cancer. It means accepting that life is different and that you can find another way to live your life with the changes. This stage also comes and goes as you face different challenges along the long journey.

Over time, researchers have recognized a sixth stage of grief: finding meaning. This stage is about finding a path forward after loss. Whether we are talking about death or the multiple losses you have experienced with cancer, seeking meaning helps you make sense of grief. Finding meaning in loss will be a personal challenge for each individual. This does not happen quickly, and you might never understand why you have had to manage cancer. You also might not feel that the losses have been worth the cost of what you have lost and endured. I am not saying your cancer was a test, a lesson, a gift, or a blessing. It is just what has happened in your life, and only you can find your own meaning. As loss is part of all our lives, we must try to find strength from our losses and allow the fear and suffering to lead us back to loving others and ourselves.

Can you recognize which phase of grief you might be experiencing right now? How do these stages continue to change for you? Do you know what situations in your treatment cause you to move from one stage to another?

As difficult as it is to speak about death, society is beginning to do so. Dr. Atul Gawande, in *Being Mortal* (2017), discusses the lack of control we have over life's circumstances. Getting to be the author of your life means getting control of what you do with those circumstances. He refers to this as autonomy. Medicine has made remarkable strides in extending life and enabling us to reach old age. There is much we can do to extend the quantity and quality of our lives. Clearly, your perspective about what is important to you changes as you become more aware through aging or illness of the limited time you might have left. Defining what is important to you as you age and facing your mortality give you the chance to shape your story, which is essential to creating meaning in your life. An authentic death is more about dying with the same values you have lived with. Most of us have the same concerns at the end of our lives.

We all want to avoid suffering. It is important to separate pain from suffering. Consider this quote: "Pain is inevitable, but suffering is optional." We have made great medical strides in managing physical pain. Suffering is more of an emotional experience involving loss of purpose and meaning.

Most of us want to be with those we love when we are at the end of our lives. This need can also extend to being able to decide whom you do not want around you at this special time.

Being mentally aware is the desire we have to be as present and in control as possible.

Not being a burden on others is a hope we all hold. This is a concern I have heard from many women, even at diagnosis. Being able to accept dependency on others is not an easy process for anyone. Accepting our vulnerability is a difficult but necessary learning for us all. It is a lot easier to be the giver than the taker for most women. Being able to ask and receive from others requires you to accept your vulnerability and needs. It is not a sign of weakness.

There are five simple phrases one can speak at the end of life that are a powerful means to help complete a relationship and allow others to come together. Can you imagine yourself being able to speak these words at the end of your life to those who matter to you?

I forgive you. Forgive me. Thank you. I love you. Goodbye.

You don't have to wait until death to express these words. There is always potential for growth and change for each of us at each moment. Acknowledging death helps you refocus on how to live more fully and with more joy because you know you don't have all the time in the world. Do it today, not tomorrow.

Another pioneer in this field is Stephen Levine, who wrote *A Year to Live* (1998). He asks us to confront our fear of death by living as if this year were our last one. As he states, death takes people unawares. He provides powerful ways to explore how you can choose to open yourself up to the life you have. Socrates recommended that we should "always be occupied in the practice of dying." In many cultures and spiritual practices, it is considered an act of wisdom to prepare for death throughout life. Many believe that preparing for death is one of the most profoundly healing acts of a lifetime. Confronting our life and death with mercy and awareness can restore our heart. The simple message is that we must not wait until we are at the end of life to live authentically according to our beliefs and values.

There continues to be more attention and information on death awareness and education. As with many social issues, artists lead with creative ways to expose us to difficult issues. In February 2011, Candy Chang, a New Orleans artist, was struggling with the loss of someone she loved. On the side of an abandoned building, she made a wall on which people could write in chalk:

Before I die, I want to _____.

Since that time, there are now a thousand walls in seventy-three countries, with messages translated into thirty-six languages.

Taking the time to sort out what is really important to you is life-affirming. Thinking about your bucket list can help you begin to define what is really important to you now.

What would you write on this wall?

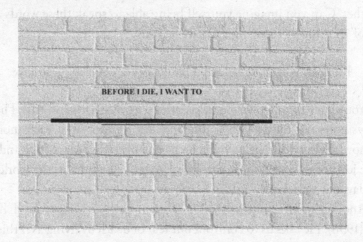

As strange as it might seem, there are even death cafés all over the world where people come together to talk about death. Facing death connects us to our sense of a common humanity. Perhaps we really are moving toward the understanding that death is our birthright, as every form of life dies.

When you think about dying, you probably have many different thoughts about the details of who, what, where, and when. Steven Spiro, a monk who teaches at Snowflower Sangha, a Buddhist retreat in Wisconsin, has compiled a directive that can help you to think about details that might be important to you in the dying process.

Tool: Advanced Directive for Conscious Dying

A. The People

1. Whom do you most want to be with you?
2. Are there any people you do not wish to have present?
3. Name those you'd like to personally contact by phone, the internet, or other means regarding your situation and condition.
4. What message would you like to be sent out to friends and family upon your death?
5. Would you prefer to have others present with you as much as possible, as little as possible, or somewhere in between?
6. When your time of death comes, would you prefer to be alone or with company?
7. Would you like someone to conduct a vigil for you so you are not alone?
8. Would you like to appoint a person or persons to be the facilitators for your spiritual care?
9. Are there any relationships to which you want to bring to resolution through forgiveness, honesty, embracing, or other means?
10. List those to whom you would like to express your blessings, advice, gratitude, and love in person or by other means.

B. The Setting

1. Describe the physical setting in which you'd prefer to die.

2. Describe the details in the room. These might include lighting, decorations, photographs, artwork, incense, flowers, furnishings, and more.

3. Are there special garments, jewelry, blankets, wraps, and so on that you would like yourself or others to wear?

C. The Content

1. List readings, poetry, scripture, and prayers that would be helpful for you. These can be read live or prerecorded and played as needed.

2. List some of your favorite songs, chants, and music that could be performed live for you or prerecorded to be played as needed.

3. List other activities that could be useful to you, such as massage, energy work, visualizations, communion, movements, postures, art making, and so on.

4. What is your desire as far as the optimal level of pain medication for you? To what degree are you willing to sacrifice comfort for awareness? At what point do you want pain medication if it begins to interfere with your level of consciousness?

5. How strictly do you want your wishes to be adhered to by your loved ones? Do you want them to do exactly as you wish even if they feel uncomfortable? Do you want your loved ones to do what brings them the most peace? Or is your preference somewhere in between?

D. Your Intentions

1. Describe your views on death and dying. What would you like your loved ones to know about your life and death? You could write this as a message to your survivors.

Jane, a sixty-two-year-old divorced mother of two adult daughters, had exhausted all the possible treatments for her metastatic disease. Her body was unable to tolerate any further interventions, and she had accepted that she was actively dying. She had always wanted to die at home. Her sunroom looked out over the river and her garden, which had always been a source of joy and peace for her. Hospice was arranged at home, and the medical support was in place. Jane was a strong-willed woman who had always maintained her sense of dignity. She was clear that she did not want to physically suffer or struggle with loss of control or vulnerability. She chose to have the level of her pain medication regulated to keep her comfortable. Her daughters struggled with her lack of ability to communicate with them and wanted the medication reduced so they could have more time with her.

When I visited Jane at her home, Jane wanted and needed to let go. For her, the pain medication allowed her to die with the self-respect she valued. Her daughters were, with some time and understanding, able to accept the final needs of their mother. Jane needed them to let go and allow her to die on her own terms. The legacy she left them was of a strong woman who charted her path throughout life and death with determination and grace.

In reading this chapter, can you sense any change in the way you are thinking and feeling about death? You might be more aware of how unready you are to address some or any of these issues. Do not feel discouraged. You can only be where you are right now in your emotional strength to tackle this challenge. I only ask that you focus on what is important to you to increase your sense of meaning and purpose each day. As with all aspects of fear, take small steps in the hope of moving forward toward whatever goal you want to set. Seek whatever support you need to feel stronger and clearer about yourself and your needs.

Identify Your Spiritual Needs

Lessons Learned from My Patients

I cannot live without hope, but what I hope for changes as my life changes.

When we think about being unable to find a physical cure, we often speak of a hopeless situation. I would like you to redefine and think about hope in a slightly different way. Hope is not the same as optimism. Hope is about being willing to open your mind and heart to something because it is good. The feeling of hope is not always joyful; rather, it is being willing to work toward a future you desire.

Even when there are limited or no options for a physical cure, there must be some focus on what brings you hope. Perhaps being able to speak to a special person, see the sunset, attend a special event, or hear some beautiful music might motivate one to live one more day with hope, presence, and awareness.

Without hope, there is no life. Even if the focus must be small and limited, it is vital to have a sense of hope. Most women diagnosed with breast cancer live long, full, and meaningful lives. They are far removed from being in a terminal phase of life. Even if setbacks might occur on your cancer journey, identifying what sparks hope for you is vital.

When the world says, "Give up," hope whispers, "Try it one more time."

—Anonymous

There is no hope unmingled with fear and no fear unmingled with hope.

—Baruch Spinoza

Hope is that thing with feathers that perches in the soul and sings the tune without words and never stops ... at all.

—Emily Dickinson

Hope is a feeling and emotion that can be hard to hold on to when you are afraid and unsure of your future health and well-being. Hope is vital for life, yet what you hope for often changes, depending on the circumstances of your life. Cancer has most likely altered how you approach hope. Most everyone begins with a hope for a cure—the absence of any physical evidence of cancer. If you have had a reoccurrence or must continue to seek out treatment to control your cancer, you can still find ways to identify what you hope for, given that you might have to live with and beyond cancer. I realize this can be a huge challenge if you have been struggling with pain and disability and the disappointment of limited treatment choices.

Dr. Anthony Scioli has developed a hope scale (www.gainhope.com) that focuses on a four-channel emotional network to tune in to hope. Let's check out these channels to search for hope.

Tool: Channels for Hope

- *The Mastery Channel.* It helps to feel a sense of control and have a clearly defined goal. A focus on what you can do now will increase your sense of personal power. Try to imagine someone you have or would like to have as a support person. Ask yourself, "What would my role model do?" See in your mind's eye this person addressing your issue and helping you see a way forward. What would they say to you, and how would they encourage you?

- *The Attachment Channel.* Feeling a sense of connection and trust with others increases your sense of hope. While walking down the street, make eye contact with and smile at the people you pass. Keep track of the positive responses. Some might not look back at you, but many will receive and appreciate your positive energy. Consider inviting someone of a different faith or ethnicity for coffee. Disclose something personal but appropriate about yourself, and see if the other person responds in kind. It takes time to trust, but being open increases the possibilities. Yes, it is a risk to reach out, but it is also a risk to your well-being to stay closed off and alone.

- *The Survival Channel.* The stress of illness requires coping tools for mind, body, and spirit. Try practicing any of the tools provided in the guide to help you cope. Again, just take one small step to begin, and build up your toolbox with what helps you on your road to healing.

- *The Spiritual Channel.* It is vital to create a sense of meaning and faith, which are the building blocks of hope. Actively expose yourself to music, art, dance, prayer, and nature to stimulate the regions of your brain that create a sense of wonder or oneness. Find a practice, such as prayer, meditation, dance, yoga, or walking mindfully, that opens you to the energy that brings a sense of your worth and value. Try practicing random acts of kindness to get out of your own head and into the act of giving and connecting to others with the kindness of your own spirit.

Which channel do you need to tune in to first to build your hope?

In thinking about end of life, we often think about the resources or possessions we want to leave to others. As opposed to a legal will, I believe an ethical will is one valuable way to communicate to others what is important to you. You don't need to be dying to write an ethical will, which is an ancient tradition initially seen in biblical times. It can be written at different stages of your life. Some of the common themes seen in modern ethical wills are

- important spiritual values,
- important personal values and beliefs,
- hopes and blessings for future generations,
- life lessons, and
- forgiving others or asking for forgiveness.

Dr. Barry Baines, author of *Ethical Wills* (2006), has been one of the strongest proponents for the use of ethical wills to preserve and pass on your values, beliefs, and hopes to your family and community. He suggests different methods to approach writing your ethical will.

The online resource www.everplans.com offers good suggestions to help you begin.

Tool: How to Write an Ethical Will

Think about the questions you might have for someone in your family who is deceased. Imagine one of your family members fifty years from now wanting to know about you. What might they want to know?

Start with a blank piece of paper. As with a journal, write down your thoughts, feelings, and experiences, and over time, specific themes will become clear. You can also save quotes or pictures that are meaningful to provide a direction for your thoughts.

- Start with an outline, and list items you want to use.
- Try a guided writing exercise. Ask yourself questions to help yourself define what is important to you. Consider the following:

> From my parents and grandparents, I learned …
> Life has taught me …
> I am grateful for …
> My most meaningful memory is of …

This is not an easy task, but it can be an amazing gift to those who care about you. You do not have to be dying to leave this legacy and gift to those you love. Your values and beliefs can be a priceless legacy to future generations. What you have to say is important. It is a gift to you as well as those who receive it.

An example of an ethical will might be the following:

> Dear beloved family,
>
> As I am growing older and thinking about the end of my life, I do not have the answers for all of life's tough questions. I do, however, want to leave you with some thoughts that I hope will support, guide, and enrich you. I feel blessed to have had you in my life and hope I have shown you clearly the love I have for each of you.
>
> I have spent my life trying (not always well) to live according to some basic principles. The first is being honest in whatever I do or say. I have worked to be responsible and

someone who can be counted on. When I have committed, I have always tried to follow through. I have tried to be caring, show compassion to others, and not hold on to anger, as I have learned that it can make me feel sick. I guess my feelings are evident, because my emotions show on my face! I have not always been patient, and when anxious, I can be irritable. For this, I ask your forgiveness.

You have given me a lifetime of amazing memories. Being together, especially traveling to new destinations, has been a source of excitement and joy. Seeing the world through my granddaughters has opened my eyes to the wonder of living each moment. They have been a true blessing to me. I only regret that I will not be able to see them grow into adulthood and make their mark as amazing young women.

My hope is that each of you will continue to find what brings you meaning and purpose in your daily life. I hope you will always continue to be open to learning, as I believe we must always try to grow and change. I pray that when you remember me, your heart will feel full of the love I leave each of you.

Mom

Will you commit to taking a seat and thinking about your conversation with loved ones? Are you ready to begin the legacy of writing your ethical will?

Leaving Your Legacy

Many years ago, I learned of a program in California called Mothers' Living Stories, which trained volunteers to go into the homes of women with breast cancer who wanted to share and record their stories for their families. Many of these women were in the final stages of their disease and wanted to leave their legacy, especially for their children. Although the program is no longer operational, the desire to leave our mark and identity on the lives of those we love is important and basic to us all.

A legacy project can take many different forms. Some of the ideas used include audio or video recordings, a genealogy, recipe boxes, an autobiography, or a collage or album. Some might choose to write cards for special future occasions. The choices are as individual as each person. Although being seriously ill is a powerful motivator to think about your legacy, remember that you have an opportunity to communicate your thoughts, values, and identity each and every day. You do not have to be at the end of your life to value what you can give to those you love.

One of our basic human needs is for generativity. This is the notion that your life has stood for something and has had some influence that will transcend and continue past your death. As we become more physically ill and come closer to accepting our death, dignity for and about oneself is part of the healing process. You must try to find a way to maintain the feeling that although you are ill, your essence of who you are is still relevant and intact. You must hold on to the identity you have created through the many different roles in your life. What have been your achievements? What has given you a sense of pride in what you have done? How will you leave a mark that your life had meaning and purpose? Hopefulness is about your ability to find that meaning and purpose. It is healing to find your sense of meaning and purpose. Many fear the burden and challenges of their illness on those they love. Being able to talk about issues and prepare others for a life without you is a gift to those who love you.

You need empathic, nonjudgmental, encouraging, and respectful care to move toward healing at the end of life. These are the same qualities of self-care you must bring to your life as you move forward each day on your road beyond breast cancer.

I cannot offer you a direct road map to finding your exit ramp. There are no bigger questions than those that surface around death. What happens when we die? Are we more than our physical bodies? Who are you as a human being, and how did you come to be here? What is this life you have, and how do you want to use it? Many find answers in their religious, spiritual, or cultural communities to support them in this journey. Established religious practice can be a vehicle to feel a sense of wholeness in one's soul. Prayers and rituals can provide a connection to something greater than yourself. Others find that sense of connection in nature and through relationships with others.

I personally believe we are more than our physical bodies. I believe we each have an essence—a soul or spirit—that lives on as long as anyone who loved us is alive. My connection to those I have lost throughout my life is maintained by my ongoing memories and feelings. I believe the key to facing our fear of dying is through love and caring. Love without judgment is the greatest buffer against fear.

> Love is eternal—love never dies. Spirit never dies. It is eternal, dynamic, evolving, unfolding, and changing. Love expresses itself in different forms and ways and at different times, but the essence quality of love never dies.

> —Satish Kumar

Lessons Learned from My Patients

Each of us must take charge of defining what we need to live life as fully as we can for as long as possible. Life is a series of losses and changes. Death ends a life, not a relationship.

Watching my patients face cancer has been my lifelong course in how the human spirit can learn to cope with loss and pain. I know with certainty that walking with them on their road of fear, change, and loss has been my opportunity to practice and face my own fears and vulnerability. I have seen how physical illness is a crisis for both the body and the spirit and a turning point in one's life. You did not cause your cancer because of what you did wrong or didn't do right. It is not an opportunity or challenge that you wanted or even needed. However, you have been called into action. Disease can point the way and serve as a transition to an expanded and revitalized life. You are not responsible for getting cancer, but you are responsible for managing it and finding what is best for you to attempt to heal. Cancer can be one of the most teachable moments in your life.

Cancer can bring you to what has been called a liminal time and place. *Liminal* is from the Latin word for *threshold*. You have been thrust into a realm of loss of innocence and might no longer be the same as before. When you cross the line between health and illness, you enter into the realm of soul. This sense of soul is felt when your everyday social face drops away, and your mind cannot focus on previous preoccupations and responsibilities. Illness is a profound soul event.

Life-threatening illness has the power to cut through illusions and bring us close to the bone, maybe for the first time in our lives. Knowing we are not in control of the situation is to come close to the essence of who we are both as unique individuals and as human beings. As we can see on X-ray films, bones are the most distinct and strongest most indestructible elements in the body. So it is that adversity reveals the external and thus indestructible qualities of the soul.

—Jean Bolen, *Close to the Bone*

Committed Action Contract

I will spend at least thirty minutes by myself writing my thoughts about what a good death would look like for me.

I will identify three situations that provide me with hope and reduce my feelings of despair.

I will move forward with writing my will and medical directives so that my affairs are in order for my family.

I will begin these actions by_____ (specific date).

For life and death are one, even as the river and the sea.

—Kahlil Gibran

I hope you will take what you need and can from this chapter on the exit route. Even if you are not ready to take any specific step to address this by yourself or with others, the information is here for you when you are ready. We all fear the unknown and the uncertainty of death. Courage is not the absence of fear but the willingness to move forward in spite of it.

6

Finding Your Path Back Home

Be Open to Exploring the Questions

- Grow through challenge and change.
- Find your happiness and meaning.
- Live as if each moment matters.

> **Lessons Learned from My Patients**
> Each of you is unique and not a statistic. My hope is to help each woman redefine, rediscover, and reconnect with what really matters to her.

As I think of the many women I have worked with, I continue to be amazed at the courage they have all shown. Whatever the specifics of their diagnoses, despite their fears and sorrows, they have been fiercely determined to live as fully as they could for as long as they were able. Whether they were motivated by their desire to be with their children and loved ones or by their own thirst for life, they dug deep inside themselves and were determined to move forward. They often lived this quote:

I am not afraid of storms for I am learning to sail my ship.

—Louisa May Alcott

This chapter is written as a series of questions to consider what can help you build your ability to weather the storm of cancer and find your own unique route back home. Coming back home will probably not feel familiar or the same as before cancer. You will feel as if your home has been remodeled. Just as it takes time to make a new house a home, you will need to give yourself time to know how to live in your new surroundings. Your body, mind, and spirit will hopefully find a new balance or healing from the demands, losses, and challenges of your cancer.

Often, patients have told me that cancer has changed their lives in positive, meaningful ways. After the initial shock and challenge of treatment, many question, "What do I really want for my life?" Although I would never imply that cancer is an opportunity you ever wanted or needed, it can offer a change of direction that is powerful and important. Women speak of a greater appreciation of life, a change in what is really important, warmer and more intimate relationships, and a clearer sense of their own strengths. They recognize new possibilities or paths for their lives and spiritual development. As mentioned in chapter 2, survivors Mary Beth and René, founders of H4TG, focused their energy on building a community of young survivors to share pain as well as joy and laughter with each other. Their support group meetings, races, retreats, educational forums, and advocacy for research are all activities that build a sense of belonging, purpose, and meaning for their members. Another patient, Susan, started blogging about her journey as a cancer patient and caregiver for her spouse. She discovered she could create employment for herself through her writing skills. Others volunteer in hospitals, community organizations, churches, and synagogues. Communicating their experiences and feelings to help others is a strong motivator for these women. It is important for all of us to feel we have something of value to offer the world—whatever forms your gift might take.

Can You Grow in the Face of Cancer?

Most of you have heard the term *post-traumatic stress disorder* (PTSD). Although it was first used to describe the struggles of soldiers after battle, we now know that trauma is much more widespread in all walks of life. Trauma can be any injury, physical or emotional. You might feel that cancer treatment has been a traumatic event for you and your loved ones. Some of you have struggled more than others with symptoms severe enough to require professional psychological help. Others have been able to bounce back to where you were before the diagnosis. Some of you have even made positive psychological changes. This is called post-traumatic growth. Wherever you feel you are on this continuum of change, there are two traits that can increase your potential for post-traumatic growth. The first is to be more open to experiences, question, and reconsider your beliefs. Can you challenge seeing cancer as a crisis?

Janice, a forty-two-year-old mother of two, came to see me after her diagnosis. When Janice was twelve, her mother, at age forty-two, died of ovarian cancer. Janice's memories of that time were of confusion, fear, and isolation. She and her sister were given little information and were not prepared for their mother's death. She was determined to create a different experience for her family.

The word *cancer* was an emotional trigger for loss and death. She first needed the emotional space to grieve the loss of her mother. She spoke directly with family members to learn more about her mother's life, illness, and death. With acceptance of her own grief and fear, she was able to prepare her children for her treatment and receive needed support from family and friends. She could challenge old beliefs and write her own cancer story. Cancer did not have to be seen as a death sentence for her.

The Chinese Symbol for Crisis ≠

Danger + Opportunity

This Chinese symbol for *crisis* speaks to another way to view your cancer diagnosis. Of course, cancer was not an opportunity you sought or needed, but how you think about your illness affects your ability to move forward.

Can you think of another word to describe your current situation other than *crisis*?

The second trait for growth is to be more willing to seek out connections with others. You might need to question what you are carrying from the past that is no longer serving you and is keeping you isolated. You might recognize you must release past memories that are no longer useful anymore and forgive yourself or others. We all need alone time, but illness is isolating and creates a sense of disconnection from the rest of the world. Finding the right balance between being with others and being alone will continue to be a challenge. Only you truly know when you are isolating and avoiding others or choosing to take care of yourself by spending time alone. Too much isolation and empty space can be unhealthy for anyone. We can all benefit from being open to perceptions and ideas that differ from our own. This is how we grow and evolve as individuals.

Tool: Identify Your Growth from Cancer

- Can you identify one positive change that has happened since your diagnosis?

_____

_____

- Can you find more value in any of your relationships?

_____

_____

- Is there one way you feel stronger about yourself since your diagnosis?

_____

_____

- Is there something in your life that has become more important to you since your diagnosis?

_____

_____

Daring to Change

As you think about building your muscle of courage and resiliency, it is helpful to consider taking a risk and daring to be different. So much has changed in your life since your diagnosis that trying to create more change might seem overwhelming. However, I ask you to stretch your muscle of courage and at least take the first step to move forward.

Tool: Dares for Encouragement

- **Dare to be silent.** Silence is more than not talking. It is the space inside you that allows you to act or speak. Pause to listen before you respond, or choose to be silent and say nothing.
- **Dare to be a hero.** Any challenge can feel risky. Heroes might not always succeed, but it takes courage just to try. As Mary Pickford said, "Failure is not falling down; it is not getting up." Don't let your what-if thinking stop you from even beginning.
- **Dare to laugh.** Laughter is good medicine for both your body and your spirit. It is a mental joy and a bond with people that can bring you together.
- **Dare to feel space.** We all live in it, breathe it, and share it. Don't take it for granted. Feel the space around you with your movements, observe the openness of the horizon, and notice the way light shines on what is around you. Be aware of physical space (chapter 3), and identify your personal space and boundaries to define your needs.

- **Dare to be affluent.** Think about how you feel when you go out looking for something you want. You are open, excited, and energized to find it. Affluence is not about what is in your bank account but about being aware of what the universe can offer you and how you can move toward it.

- **Dare to be spirited.** Don't be afraid to show some energy. If you have a chance, sing to the radio or in the shower. Reach out, and give someone a hug. Smile at the next person you see. Don't be afraid and hide your spirit. Express it!

- **Dare to be different.** Just because you have always done something the same way doesn't mean it is the best or only way. What will you do to take a chance and change it up? Open up to the fresh, new, exciting feeling of change. Life is surely different from the way it was before cancer, with difficult choices. Even a small change can bring renewal and a feeling of more openness.

- **Dare to decide.** You have had to make many important decisions throughout your cancer journey. Even though there is never a guarantee, staying stuck in fear keeps you from moving forward. It's OK to be afraid, but take that small first step to take a chance.

Pick one of these dares, and choose a specific behavior to build your resiliency. What will you dare to do?

_____

_____

Life shrinks or expands in proportion to one's courage.

—Anaïs Nin

How Can You Find Happiness?

Resiliency is the ability to bounce back after illness or any misfortune or loss. You are not necessarily born with this trait, but with knowledge, determination, and support, you can build your resilient muscle. You took a first step in this building process by opening this guide. Developing your resilient muscle is the key to more happiness and meaning in your life. We know through research that happiness and a sense of meaning in your life are related. Happiness creates more meaning, and having a sense of meaning in your life creates more happiness.

Happiness ← → Sense of Meaning

It is a myth that finding meaning in your life is a mystery or difficult. You just have to look around and identify the behaviors, situations, and relationships that bring you an internal feeling of joy. You then commit to paying attention to them in your daily life.

Cancer can challenge you to discover your reason to live with a will that is determined to do so, faith that it is possible, and wise choices about what to do. It doesn't require deep thinking or reflection. Finding time when you are totally absorbed, engaged, and fascinated in what you are doing is to find soul-nourishing time—moments when you lose track of time, let go of everything else, and are absorbed in the present moment. These are called moments of flow. Searching too hard for meaning is not the way to find it. We also know that happiness comes when you use your strengths to contribute to the happiness of others.

Can you remember a time when you were lost in the moment and fully engaged in a nourishing way?

_____

_____

Who in your life today might benefit from some loving attention? What is one small gesture you can make to show them they matter?

_____

_____

A pleasant life of enjoyment can bring you happiness. You want your body to feel comfortable and without pain, to share good times with loved ones, and to have a safe and secure home. Sometimes, however, we develop not-so-healthy ways to feel enjoyment, such as eating poorly, spending too much, or engaging in alcohol or substance abuse. You must learn to nurture your body so that it can serve you to fulfill your deepest desires.

Learning to live with more mindfulness of the present moment can increase your experience of fullness and enjoyment. Although there is no guarantee the present moment always will be pleasant, the chance to feel what is good and meaningful is lost when you are not aware of what is right in front of you. Don't forget to stop to smell the roses! Be aware of how you can bring your five physical senses into your daily life to increase your pleasure and joy.

Identify a time when you felt enjoyment or pleasure. What made that time so pleasant? How does thinking about it now make you feel as you remember?

Psychology now recognizes the value of focusing on positive emotions rather than just on what is wrong or missing for each of us. The PERMA theory, developed by Dr. Martin Seligman, can help you increase well-being.

Tool: Increase Your Happiness

- *P: Positive emotions.* Think about when you feel pride and excitement. When was the last time you were truly happy about what you had done or were going to do?
- *E: Engagement.* What kinds of activities draw you in and build your interest? Can you remember the last time you lost track of time because you were so engaged and involved in what you were doing?
- *R: Relationships.* Other people matter, and how you cultivate kindness toward them matters. Where and how do you connect with others at work and home, with friends, or in a romantic way?

How can you be more emotionally present and engaged with others?

- *M: Meaning and purpose.* It is often impossible to try to answer the *why* questions, such as "Why did this happen to me?" Opening yourself up to seeking something greater than yourself can bring a sense of meaning and purpose. Is there some need in your personal life or larger community that you can commit your time and energy to?

- *A: Accomplishments.* Try to identify one way you might seek success or mastery. It can be a small goal, but aiming for success moves you forward toward the possibility of happiness.

Tool: Evaluate What Matters to You

To find a greater sense of happiness, you must be able to identify what matters to you.

Below is a chart that lists ten areas of your life to help you sort out what matters most to you. Number them as to their importance from 1 to 10, with 1 being the most important. The second column evaluates how much you are manifesting or living that value. Again, number them from 1 to 10, with 1 the most important. Subtract the two numbers for each value.

VALUE	IMPORTANCE	MANIFESTATION	DIFFERENCE
INTIMATE			
FRIENDS			
WORK			
SPIRITUALITY			
LEISURE			
CARETAKING			
EDUCATION			
HEALTH			
FAMILY			
COMMUNITY			

Are you focusing on the areas of your life that matter most to you? Can you choose one small step to adjust how you spend your time to reflect what is more important to you?

_____

_____

Tool: How You Want to Spend Your Precious Time

As you identify what is important to you, how you take charge of your time is vital to finding a healthy balance. You probably function on autopilot most of the time, doing what you think you need to do. Part of taking charge and directing your life is to figure out what really matters and what you do with your time.

This exercise will help you sort out how you are spending your time. Are you filling your days with an ongoing list of *shoulds* or making choices to live in a way more aligned with what matters most to you? How you commit your precious time is important to living a life that is true to yourself.

Activities common to your week	Activities you spend the most time on	Activities most meaningful to you

In column 1, list five to ten activities common to your week.

In column 2, rank the activities, with the most time spent as the first on the list and so on.

In column 3, order the activities in terms of what is most meaningful to you to live a full life. (You might have activities in this column not listed in column 1 or 2.)

Now draw a line between the similar items in column 2 and column 3. Are those lines straight or diagonal? Are you spending time doing activities that are meaningful to you?

What have you learned about how you are spending your time?

You might be saying to yourself, "I can't do what I want to do because of the needs of my family. There are things that have to happen, and I need to do them." Certainly there are obligations you have, but there is surely some wiggle room.

Here is an example of a patient who found some wiggle room to help her cope during her treatment process. Maria, forty-five years old, had completed her chemotherapy and was going to her radiation treatments. She was the only caregiver living in the area for her widowed mother, who was in poor health and depressed. Though her mother knew that Maria was in treatment, she continued to make demands on her attention and time. Maria found herself becoming resentful and overwhelmed. She came to recognize that she had to reach out to her siblings for help. Always quick to take on the caregiver role in the family, she understood that as long as she alone took sole responsibility, others did not have to do so. She determined the cost and kind of care her mother needed and contacted each of her siblings.

Although Maria continued to be the child who organized the care for her mother, her siblings were able to share in providing the financial and emotional resources for their mother. The challenges continued, but Maria felt more support from the extended family and less resentful. She no longer felt like the victim.

What is one small change you can make to spend more time doing what makes your life more meaningful?

Tool: Planning Your Time for a Healthy Mind

How you spend your time is not only important for your emotional well-being and physical health, but also to maintain a well functioning brain. Dr. David Rock and Dr. Dan Siegel (2012) developed an informational graphic to help you understand how you might organize your daily schedule to build connections between your mind, body, and spirit for optimal health. There is no set amount of time you should spend on each of these seven activities, but try to find a way to include each of the ingredients in your daily meal plan.

The Healthy Mind Platter

The Healthy Mind Platter, for Optimal Brain Matter

- *Time in*. In chapter 4, we discussed mindfulness. This is time to move inward and focus your attention on the present moment without judgment. This can build your ability to focus and expand your awareness with more self-compassion.
- *Connecting time*. This is time to reach out to others. As discussed in chapter 3, you cannot travel the winding road of cancer alone. Although time alone can feed your spirit, accepting your need to have the support of others is vital to your healing. Connecting to the rhythms of nature may also be a way to ground and steady yourself.
- *Focus time*. This is time to focus on an activity that may require some discipline. It can be reading a book, engaging in a creative activity, playing an instrument—whatever activity helps you focus your attention. Focus and attention can be challenging when

you are managing side effects from treatment. You may need to schedule only a short amount of time and then increase it as you feel physically stronger. This focusing can help improve memory and your sense of appreciation for the activity.

- *Play time.* This is time to be spontaneous and take that laughter pill prescribed in chapter 2. Being able to let go with others and play in the moment with a sense of freedom from judgment is life-affirming for us all.

- *Physical time.* Cancer fatigue is real and challenging. As discussed in chapter 2, you just have to move. Remember, think beyond exercise, and think about moving your body. Create energy to feel your life force. Think of the image of moving forward to lift your mood as well as strengthen your brain.

- *Downtime.* Find time to just be and let your mind wander. This is different from being mindless and distracted, as discussed in chapter 4. This is time to just be in the present moment and relax. You might want to watch a show, listen to some music, watch the sunset, or just listen to the birds.

- *Sleep time.* Clearly, you know how important sleep is to your physical healing. Chapter 2 discusses how to practice good sleep hygiene. Adequate, quality sleep is also vital to the health of the neurons in your brain and the way you process calories. Giving your brain time to restore and refresh through sleep is vital to your emotional and physical health.

Will you take a serving of each of these plates and plan your meal today to put yourself at the head of your table? Think of specific behaviors to serve on each plate of the platter. This is guilt-free nutritional eating for your mind, body, and spirit.

The Big *C*s in Cancer

Years ago, people avoided even mentioning the word *cancer* in polite society. People used to talk about the so-called big *C*. The disease created much fear that led to even more isolation and trauma for patients. We know that facing cancer and all its challenges is the way to heal. I believe there are some big *C*s that are important to discuss, as they can increase your chance of moving forward. Avoiding important issues in your life can clutter the closet of your mind and keep you feeling stuck and bogged down. Imagine your mind as a closet or drawer that needs cleaning, and let's talk about the *C*s that need attention.

Tool: The Big *C*s for Moving Forward

1. *Confidence.* What are some of the things you want to do that you have never done? Be aware if you are telling yourself, "I can't do that." Comparison to others only limits you. Challenge any fearful self-talk that is preventing you from taking that first step. Think about positive successes you have had in your life, no matter how small they seem. Can you remember how you felt when you accomplished those goals? What would help you to take just that first step?

Success consists of getting up just one more time than you fall.

—Oliver Goldsmith

2. *Commitment* and *consistency.* What is one behavior you have started and not finished? Is there a project waiting for you to pick back up? Be honest with yourself, and own the effort you must bring to your goal. What are the steps needed to move from thought to action? What specific behavior (e.g., exercise, healthy eating, or self-care) have you tried to change and not continued? Continuing to keep your goal in focus is a process you must commit to over and over again. There is always something that can throw you off your stated goal. Consider making a schedule you know you can keep with however small a commitment of time or space to help you stay on course.

3. *Clarity.* What are some behaviors you want to stop and are not stopping? Have you picked up some bad habits that need weeding out? A clear vision of your goal is vital to making any change.

Choose a specific behavior you want to change, and define an alternative behavior to counter that bad habit. Keep the steps small when you take it forward. Remember, if you can change a behavior for at least twenty-one days, there is a good chance you can build that new goal into a new habit (e.g., "I will put less pressure on myself to accomplish tasks and will give myself fifteen minutes each day to relax").

4. *Courage.* Are there some things you want to say and have not said? Courage is like a muscle that must be exercised. With whom do you have unfinished business? Fear and risk go together. Sometimes it helps to ask yourself, "What is the worst thing that can happen if I _____?" Think about someone you respect who has shown the courage of their convictions. Use some of the communication tools in chapter 3 to think about what truth you want to speak and how you want to speak it.

5. *Coaching* and *competence.* Is there something you want or need to learn and never learned? At diagnosis, you face a lot of questions and new information. We all need a mentor or guide to help us when we face uncertainty. Being open to looking and asking others is necessary. You must gather the information you need to make hard decisions about treatment or other issues in your life. Use your judgment to filter information you read or hear. Once you make a decision, do not keep questioning yourself. Do your homework when you need to make a decision, and then trust your decision. As you move forward toward more health, you might also gain interest in new areas of learning, which can further enlarge your life.

6. *Community.* Do you feel anger toward someone in your world that you have not expressed? Who or what is taking up a lot of rent-free space in your mind? Do you need to go directly to that person or situation to resolve the issue? Perhaps you need to limit contact with that source of negative energy while you are trying to heal. Forgiveness toward yourself or others might also be the way

to move forward. Remember, forgiveness is not forgetting, and it can be a gift to yourself when you are ready to let go of the hurt.

When you are ready to choose a behavior or habit you want to change, use this model to help you begin. Which *C* needs attention first?

_____

_____

Tool: How to Know If You Are Really Ready to Change

- Pick one behavior you want to change. For example, maybe your nutrition is poor, you don't exercise, or you get angry too easily with others.
- Write down clearly the behavior you want to change.
- Write down how often you behave this way. Create a record to track where you are starting and how much change you can make.
- List the advantages of making this change, and know that changing is more important than not changing.

If you can do the above, you are ready to begin to make a change. The following is important.

Tool: Steps for Changing an Unhealthy Habit

1. Identify what leads up to your unhealthy habit. What specific feelings or situations lead to this habit? For example, do you eat poorly when you are bored or alone? Do you stay up too late and not get enough sleep?
2. Describe your habit. What do you do step by step? When, where, and with whom do you do this behavior? Perhaps you only do it when alone, but define the specific details.
3. Practice daily some form of stress relief while you are making this change. Change is hard, so you need coping tools.

4. Know the situations that bring about your habit. Try to identify your mood and what causes you to begin your habit. Knowledge is power.

5. Develop something else you can do whenever you have the urge to start your problematic habit. Choose something you can do often and as frequently as you need to. This alternative behavior should be something you can do for several minutes. It must be something completely different from your habit. For example, get up, go to another room, and occupy yourself instead of going to the refrigerator to snack before bedtime. When you want to express anger, use your breath to slow down and pause. Count to ten before you choose to speak.

6. Rehearse your healthy response each day.

7. Enlist one or two people you trust to help you change. Let them know you need positive feedback, not criticism. We all need praise for our efforts.

8. List the situations you might be avoiding because of your limiting habit. Plan when you are ready to put yourself in those situations to show yourself the improvement you can make.

9. List the things you plan to do and dates when you would like to do them.

Consider this example to help you begin to change an unhealthy habit.

I want to eat fewer desserts with sugar after dinner before I go to bed at night. I know that if I can substitute something healthy with less sugar, I can better maintain my weight, sleep better, and feel more in control.

I know that I eat at night to fill the unstructured time after dinner and before bedtime. I look at dessert as a treat for myself after a long day, especially when I am tired. I want to find healthier ways to treat myself other than sweets. I need to change what I do after dinner to create the space and time to think before I start eating sweets. I will try to commit to take five to ten minutes after dinner to make a thoughtful choice of what I really want. I will go into the den and sit in my comfortable chair before I decide about dessert. I might want to have something sweet, but I will be more mindful of what I really want and how much I want to eat. I will ask my husband to help me remember to stop before I have dessert. I will begin this next week on Sunday, December 13.

Record of My After-Dinner Eating Behavior

Sunday 12/6	Monday 12/7	Tuesday 12/8	Wednesday 12/9	Thursday 12/10	Friday 12/11	Saturday 12/12
1 piece of cake	2 cookies	½ chocolate bar	1 apple	1 frozen yogurt bar	1 piece of cake	1 cup of flavored tea
Sunday 12/13	Monday 12/14	Tuesday 12/15	Wednesday 12/16	Thursday 12/17	Friday 12/18	Saturday 12/19
1 banana	1 sugar-free muffin	1 piece of cake	1 navel orange	1 large apple	Decaf coffee w/ cinnamon	1 cup flavored tea

Change is hard, but will you pick one limiting habit you want to change for your health and healing? Remember, just pick one specific small behavior to begin.

It is easier to act your way into a new way of thinking than think your way into a new way of acting.

—Harry Stack Sullivan

_____

_____

I know this guide constantly challenges you to create change and find the strength to take charge of your cancer. A fighting spirit has always been the route to better outcomes in cancer. You cannot allow yourself to stay stuck as a victim to this disease. Although you will not have the strength all the time, you may find some of the following suggestions can help you become more of a warrior. *The Warrior's Guide to Getting Well* by psychologists Jeanne Achterberg, PhD, and Frank Lawlis, PhD, was presented at a workshop in 1989. With their permission, I am sharing this with you because it speaks directly on how to be a warrior and care for yourself when you are managing the challenges of cancer.

This list was written to help anyone who has been diagnosed with the unknowable, the unthinkable, the awful, and the so-called incurable.

1. Try not to panic. You will become your worst enemy if you do.
2. Find a quiet, healing, sacred place, and go there. This might take a week or a year. Ask the most spiritual part of your being, and listen.
3. Take time to think about this and what you want to do. A warrior does not go off half-cocked.
4. Find at least one friend or advocate you can talk to when you are going crazy who can be positive when you feel doomed and can listen when your head is buzzed with problems.
5. Kindly tell all negative-thinking people to get lost while you are going through this.
6. Assess your belief system. What do you believe? What is happening inside you? How serious is this, and what will it take for you to get well?
7. Gather information, and keep an open mind. All who offer to treat you or give you advice have their lives invested in what they tell you. A warrior stands back and listens thoughtfully.
8. Go hire your healing team. Remember, you hired them, and they are performing a service for you. Make sure they talk to each other. You, the warrior, are in command.
9. Don't let anyone talk you into treatment you (a) don't believe in or (b) don't understand. Keep asking questions.
10. Don't agree to any diagnostic test unless you understand why it is being ordered.
11. Sing your own song, write your own story, and take your own journey through this. Who are you, and what does this disease have to do with your presence on this earth?
12. Love yourself. Ask moment by moment whether what surrounds you is nurturing and life-giving. If the answer is no, back off.

13. Never forget: Everything cures somebody, and nothing cures everybody. There are no simple answers to complex issues, such as why people get sick in the first place.

14. A warrior is not intimated by the overbearing world of medicine or new-age know-it-alls but can take the best of all worlds.

15. As a warrior, you can teach gentleness and compassion to any doctor or nurse. Tell them you need your mind, body, and soul to be nurtured in order to get well. If they are not up to it, you can find someone or someplace that is.

How will you stand up and be the warrior you can be to move your healing journey forward?

_____

_____

Some Parting Words on Your Route Home

My work as a psychologist has provided me the opportunity to intimately share with women and their families the challenges of cancer. I have tried to simply be a guide who travels by their side. My role in the healing process is to try to support others to find the healing power within them. My patients continue to be my teachers in this course of life, loss, and challenge. I have seen how cancer can be a crisis for the body, mind, and spirit when one crosses the threshold between health and illness. Life-threatening illness, such as cancer, has the power to cut through past illusions. You have lost your sense of innocence and might no longer be the same as before. Illness can be a profound soul experience and reveal the powerful qualities of your soul and spirit.

Healing from cancer is about finding a new balance for your body, mind, and spirit. Clearly, you must pay attention to your physical needs. Obviously, you must listen to your body. If not, it will just scream louder. How will you nurture your body so that it can serve you to fulfill your deepest desires? Proper breathing, healthy movement, nutrition, and sleep are behaviors you can have some control over. In a time when so much feels out of control, focusing on what is under your control is vital. Pay attention to how you can bring your senses of smell, touch, and hearing into your daily life to increase your pleasure and relaxation. Recognize and accept without blame or shame what your body has endured. I hope I have provided you some of the tools to begin to connect with your body in kinder and more compassionate ways. These are necessary tools for a lifetime.

I hope you will honor your gut instincts but also be aware of your mind's ability to lead you astray when you are afraid, angry, or grieving. You must recognize that your sense of well-being is not just your blood work but also a measure of your brain chemistry and functioning. Your physical brain is affected not only by your cancer treatment but also by the way you think. Your thoughts can keep you from locating your home base and emotional center. Your ability to calm your thoughts as well as your body will enable you to move toward your strong internal compass. Find your special form of relaxation, meditation, visualization, or connection to others to increase the power of your mind.

Although you might not be able to prevent thoughts from bubbling up inside your head, you can challenge thinking that is unhealthy for you. You are more than your thoughts. Even when life does not go the way you think it should, try changing *should* to *could*. *Should* shrinks your ability to think through a more critical lens. *Could* opens you up to possibility and choice. Although it's possible not every option will be available, challenging critical, negative thinking is the power you can bring to your life. Please remember my familiar mantra: It is not "what if" but "what now."

Focusing on the present might not always be easy, but the present moment is under your control. How can you slow down to find your own center and connect with the larger universe? Use some of the relaxation tools to find that calm sense of peace. Time becomes even more precious after a cancer diagnosis. Taking charge of how you spend your time is the way you value yourself. How can you balance your time for work, time for contemplation, and time for fun? Make time each day to be alone with yourself. Turn off the external noise, and move inward. Bringing mindfulness through meditation, walking, yoga, or prayer creates an inner space to let silence be a partner in your healing. Nurturing yourself both physically and emotionally is the road to healing.

Focus on small behaviors you can change to feel less vulnerable and afraid. Be aware of how your critical self-talk keeps you from even beginning to try to create change. Having self-compassion and accepting yourself as you are in this moment can tame the inner critic in your mind. You do not need to be perfect to be worthy of love. Just stretch, and take that first small step.

The role of spirit is another important path in finding your route back home. Your spirit is the part of you that is connected to something bigger than yourself. Whether it is a higher power or a sense of community and the connection we all share, it helps you recognize that you do not have to travel home alone if you need help. Accepting your need for help will enable you to find and feel the support that is available. Recognizing how your physical and emotional wounds affect your daily life can begin your process of creating change. Identifying what you need to hold on to and what you need to let go of will help you travel more directly back to your home base: you.

The stark awareness of your mortality will accompany you on this journey. Navigating what you want and communicating it to those who matter to you is a difficult but empowering part of the journey. It is a gift of love to those who care about you and want to respect what you want. Let them know what you want so they can give you that final gift when the time arrives.

Try to tune in each day to remember it is good to be alive. Remember what has brought you peace, and feel what it is like to be alive. Having gratitude for difficulties that could have happened but did not happen is one way to build your spiritual bank. Know what you are carrying from your past that is no longer serving you in the present. What role does forgiveness toward yourself or others need to play in your healing? Focus on experiences that create a sense of awe. Seek out where you can find that sense of experiences that are larger than life. Is it in nature, art, or connection with others? As difficult as it might seem when life challenges you, remember, you cannot and do not need to manage it alone. Find the support you need to help you heal with those you trust.

Angeles Arrien, PhD, in *The Four-Fold Way* (1993), has four rules for living, which are some of my favorite guidelines I have shared over the years.

- Show up. You have chosen to read this guide, so give yourself some credit.
- Pay attention—not only to what is presented to you but also to your own inner voice and truth. Listen to what your inner self really wants so you can move forward on your unique path.
- Tell the truth. Be honest with yourself and others to build trust in your decisions and increase your connection to others.
- Don't be attached to the results. This one is the most challenging. Letting go of the results is difficult, especially when you want to be healthy and free of cancer. Doing the best you can is all you can attempt. Whatever the future holds, having self-compassion and cultivating real love will help reduce fear.

I hope this guide has been a useful companion on your journey beyond breast cancer. I have tried to provide you with many of the tools my patients have found helpful. However, you must decide the direction you follow. You are not alone on this road, but your inner compass and navigation must follow your own heart and inner truth. You are in the driver's seat and must chart your own unique route. My hope is and will always be for your healing.

Here is the last sample action contract. Please commit yourself to using this guide to help yourself find your route back home to your own healing. Hopefully you will want to return to this guide at different points on your journey. No matter how small a change you can make, just begin. Every step toward gaining more self-awareness will move you forward and assist in your healing process. Remember to value what you are already doing in your life that is healthy and loving. Be compassionate when you feel stuck, and give yourself the grace you would give to others you love. Thank you for your time and effort. Let this be a strong beginning to your future health.

Committed Action Contract

I will nurture my body today by _____.

I will challenge my critical self-voice about my limitations with an authentic, realistic alternative thought: _____.

I will take the first step to resolve conflict with someone who is important to me:

_____.

I will create some personal time for myself each day by

_____

I will begin these changes by_____(specific date).

Although I am not a poet, I offer you my "Many Paths to Healing" poem. May you travel safely on your journey beyond breast cancer and find peace, wholeness, and love.

There are many paths to healing,
Many roads to love and life.

There is light along this journey
To guide you along your way.

The path, at times, is steep and narrow.
Your footing may not always be sure.

Turn to seek those along with you
To support the climb and soften the falls.

Tune in to the signals your body is giving you
To discover the voice of your own direction.

There are many paths to healing,
Many roads to love and life.

Tools for the Road

Chapter 1: The Uncertain Roundabout

Tools for Your Body

- Abdominal Breathing
- Mini Relaxations
- Shifting Your Awareness
- Jacobson's Relaxation Response
- Time Management
- Shifting Time

Tools for Your Mind

- The Relaxation Response
- The Relaxing Sigh: "Ahh"
- Visualization and Guided Imagery
- Your Six-Word Cancer Journey
- The STOP Tool
- Shifting Your Thoughts to Reducing Anxiety and Fear

Tools for Your Spirit

- Create Your Personal Ritual
- Moving through Fear

Chapter 2: The Rough and Lonely Road

Tools for Your Body

- Improve Your Sleep
- Food-Mood Diary
- Food-Mood Checklist

Tools for Your Mind

- Understanding Your Sadness
- Get Unhooked
- Challenge Your Thinking
- How to Write Your Personal Affirmation
- How to Take in the Good

Tools for Your Spirit

- Letting Go
- Ways to Move Forward with Forgiveness
- Steps to Forgiveness
- Building Your Hope Muscle

Chapter 3: You Are Not Traveling Alone

Tools for Your Body

- Identify Your Sexual Turnoffs
- Poisons for Your Arousal
- The CREST Tool for Improved Sexual Life

Tools for Your Mind

- Ten Steps for a Problem-Solving Win-Win Approach
- The Daily Temperature Reading

- Planning Your Time for a Healthy Mind
- The Big *C*s for Moving Forward
- How to Know If You Are Really Ready to Change
- Steps for Changing an Unhealthy Habit

Resources

Chapter 1

Books

Benson, Herbert. *The Relaxation Response*. New York: William Morrow Paperbacks, 2000.

Bourne, Edward. *The Anxiety and Phobia Workbook*. 7th ed. California: New Harbinger Press, 2020.

Brach, Tara. *Radical Acceptance Awakening the Love That Heals Fear and Shame*. London: Ebury Press, 2003.

Doumar, Alice. *Self-Nurture: Learning to Care for Yourself as Effectively as You Care for Others*. New York: Penguin Books, 2001.

Geffen, Jeremy. *The Journey through Cancer*. New York: Crown Publishing, 2000.

Graham, Linda. *Resilience*. California: New World Library, 2018.

Jacobson, Edward. *Progressive Relaxation*. Chicago: University of Chicago Press, 1938.

Notaras, Kelly. *The Book You Were Born to Write*. Carlsbad, California: Hay House Publishing, 2018.

Wehrenberg, Margaret. *The Ten Best-Ever Anxiety Management Techniques*. 2nd ed. New York: W. W. Norton and Company, 2018.

Wilson, Reid. *Don't Panic*. 3rd ed. New York: Harper Perennial, 2009.

Web Resources

https://www.soundstrue.com
https://www.newharbinger.com
https://www.healthjourneys.com
https://www.tarabrach.com
https://www.manypathstohealing.com

Chapter 2

Books

Hanson, Rick. *Buddha's Brain: The Practical Neuroscience of Happiness, Love, and Wisdom*. Oakland, California: New Harbinger Press, 2009.
———. *Hardwiring Happiness*. Pennsylvania: Harmony Press, 2013.
Korn, L. *Nutrition Essentials for Mental Health*. New York: W. W. Norton and Company, 2016.
Kushner, Harold. *When Bad Things Happen to Good People*. Norwell, Massachusetts: Anchor Press, 2007.
Luskin, Fred. *Forgive for Good*. New York: Harper One, 2003.
———. *Forgive for Love*. New York: Harper One, 2009.
Michaels, C., and M. Drozda. *Exercise for Cancer Survivors*. Victoria, Canada: Friesen Press, 2013.
Rinpoche, Sogyal. *The Tibetan Book of Living and Dying*. New York: Harper One, 2009.
Snyder, C. R. *The Psychology of Hope*. New York: Free Press, 2010.

Web Resources

https://www.hereforthegirls.org
https://www.findapsychologist.org
https://www.psychologytoday.com
https://www.sleepfoundation.org
https://www.nccn.org
https://www.myyogajournal.com

https://www.lorettalaroche.com
https://www.laughteronlinuniversity.com

Chapter 3

Books

Barbach, Lonnie. *For Yourself: The Fulfillment of Female Sexuality*. Berkeley: Penguin Books, 2000.

Brach, Tara. *Radical Compassion*. New York: Viking, 2019.

Emmons, Robert. *The Little Book of Gratitude*. Louisville, Colorado: Gaia, 2016.

Gordon, Lori. *Passage to Intimacy*. New York: Fireside, 2001.

Gottman, John. *Seven Principles for Making Marriage Work*. New York: Harmony Books, 2015.

Halprin, Sharon. *The Etiquette of Illness*. London: Bloomsbury, 2004.

Lerner, Harriet. *The Dance of Anger*. New York: Avon, 2014.

———. *Why Won't You Apologize?* New York: Gallery Books, 2017.

Maisano, Gina. *Intimacy after Breast Cancer*. New York: Square One, 2009.

McCarthy, Barry, and Emily McCarthy. *Discovering Your Couple Sexual Style*. United Kingdom: Routledge, 2009.

———. *Rekindling Desire*. 3rd ed. United Kingdom: Routledge, 2019.

Neff, Kristen. *Self-Compassion*. New York: William Morrow, 2015.

Pipher, Mary. "The Joy of Being a Woman in Her 70s." *New York Times*, January 12, 2019.

Salzberg, Sharon. *Loving-Kindness: The Revolutionary Art of Happiness*. Boulder, Colorado: Shambhala Press, 2002.

Web Resources

Rosenthal, Amy. "7 Notes on Life." 2010. https:// youtu.be/hxWglccldh4.

Olsen, Milton. "Lessons from Geese." 2010. https:// you.tu.be/UdEjL9bVcCM.

https://www.selfcompassion.org

https://www.greater good. berkeley.edu

https://www.purposebuiltfamilies.com
https://www.sharonsalzberg.com
https://www.caregiver.org

Chapter 4

Books

Brach, Tara. *Radical Compassion*. New York: Viking, 2019.

Fralich, Terry. *Five Core Skills for Mindfulness: A Direct Path to More Confidence, Joy, and Love*. Wisconsin: PESI Publishing, 2013.

Geffen, David. *Journey through Cancer*. New York: Crown Publishing, 2000.

Germer, Christopher, and Sharon Salzberg. *The Mindful Path to Self-Compassion*. New York: Guilford Press, 2009.

Hanh, Thich Nhat. *Peace Is Every Step*. New York: Bantam, 1992.

Kabat-Zinn, Jon. *Full Catastrophe Living*. New York: Delta Book, 1990.

———. *Wherever You Go, There You Are*. New York: Hiperion, 1994.

Koenig, Harold. *The Healing Power of Faith*. New York: Simon and Schuster, 2001.

Naparstek, Belleruth. *Your Sixth Sense*. San Francisco: Harper, 1997.

Neff, Kristen. *Self-Compassion*. New York: William Morrow, 2015.

Pearsall, Paul. *The Pleasure Prescription*. Alameda, California: Hunter House, 1996.

Salzberg, Sharon. *Loving-Kindness: The Revolutionary Art of Happiness*. Boulder, Colorado: Shambala Press, 2002.

Web Resources

https://www.llorettalaroche.com
https://www.mindfulnesscenter.org
https://www.calm.com
https://www.drweil.com

https://www.mrsmindfulness.com
https://www.tarabrach.com
https://www.gainhope.com

Chapter 5

Books

Baines, Barry. *Ethical Wills*. Boston: DeCapo Lifelong Books, 2006.

Blackman, Linda. *Another Morning*. California: Seal Press, 2006.

Bolen, Jean. *Close to the Bone*. San Francisco: Conari Press, 2007.

Gawande, Atul. *Being Mortal*. London: Picador, 2017.

Kessler, David. *Finding Meaning*. New York: Scribner, 2020.

Kübler-Ross, Elisabeth, and Ira Byock. *On Death and Dying*. New York: Scribner, 2014.

Levine, Stephen. *A Year to Live*. New York: Bell Tower Press, 1998.

Murdock, Diane. *The New Art of Dying*. Virginia Beach: Murdocks LLC, 2014

Web Resources

https://www.cancer.gov
https://www.conversationproject.org
https://www.mygiftofgrace.com
https://www.deathoverdinner.org
https://www.fivewishes.org
https://www.eoluniversity.com
https://www.acpdecisions.org
https://www.nhdd.org
https://www.beforeidie.cc
https://www.gainhope.com
https://www.celebrationsoflife.net
https://www.everplans.com
https://www.motherslivingstories.com
https://www.joincake.com

Chapter 6

Books

Achterberg, Jeanne. *Cancer as a Turning Point*. Audiobook. Boulder, Colorado: Sounds True, 2015.

Arrien, Angeles. *The Four-Fold Way: Walking the Path of Warrior, Teacher, Healer, and Visionary*. San Francisco: Harper One, 1993.

Blanke, Gail. *In My Wildest Dreams*. New York: Simon and Schuster, 1999.

Borysenko, Joan. *Fire in the Soul*. New York: Grand Central Publishing, 1994.

Clairborn, James, and Cherry Pedrick. *The Habit Change Workbook*. Oakland, California: New Harbinger Press, 2001.

Leshan, Lawrence. *Cancer as a Turning Point*. New York: Plume Publishing, 1994.

Lyubomirsky, Sonja. *The How of Happiness*. New York: Penguin Press, 2008.

Nin, Anaïs. *The Diary of Anaïs Nin*. Houghton Mifflin Harcourt, 1969, 1980.

Rock, David and Dan Siegel, "The Healthy Mind Platter for Optimal Brain Matter," *Neuroleadership Journal*, 2011, Page 23

Seligman, Martin. *Authentic Happiness*. New York: Atria, 2004.

Web Resources

https://www.ppc.sas.upenn.edu
https://www.viacharacter.org

Index

therapist, how to find one, 36–37
Thich Nhat Hanh, 122
thinking, challenging yours, 51
thought replacement, 22
The Tibetan Book of Living and Dying
      (Sogyal Rinpoche), 58
time
    determining how you want to
        spend yours, 174–175
    planning for a healthy mind, 176
time, shifting of, 10–11
time management, 9–10
time urgency, 109
tools
    for body, 3–4, 5–6, 9–11, 39–40,
        43–44, 76, 79–80, 82–83,
        109, 110–111, 114–115,
        143–144, 145, 146, 168–
        170, 172–177, 178–182,
        191, 192, 193, 194–195
    for mind, 12–14, 15, 19–20, 22–
        23, 48, 49–50, 51, 54–55,
        56–57, 85–86, 87–90,
        91–92, 96, 117, 118–119,
        120–122, 149–150, 153–
        154, 168–170, 172–177,
        178–182, 191, 192–193,
        193, 194–195
    for spirit, 25, 26–28, 58–60,
        61–62, 63–64, 66, 98–99,
        100–102, 103–104, 125–
        126, 127–132, 133–137,
        157–158, 159–160, 168–
        170, 172–177, 178–182,
        191, 192, 193–194, 194–195

touch
    as bridge for sexual desire, 77–78
    use of, 110–111
trauma, 166–167
trust
    as component of HEALTH, 67, 68
tunnel vision, 50

U

The Ultra Geese (movie), 104–105
uncertainty
    as creating fear, 26
    how it affects your body, 1–11
    how it affects your mind, 11–23
    your spirit and, 24–28
unworthiness, trance of, 127

V

values, 152, 158, 159, 161, 173
visualization, 13–14
Voltaire, 77

W

The Warrior's Guide to Getting Well
      (Achterberg and Lawlis),
      182–184
Weil, Andrew, 109
Whitman, Walt, 9
writing. *See* journaling

Y

A Year to Live (Levine), 151
yoga, 42

CPSIA information can be obtained
at www.ICGtesting.com
Printed in the USA
JSHW032215020423
39788JS00005B/27